Take Back Your Day

How to Hack Time Management Like a Boss

By Andrew Fine
and Michael Ashley

Take Back Your Day

Copyright © 2019 by Andrew Fine

ISBN: 9781797045955

ASIN: 1797045954

Contents

Dedication

To my wife, Sabrina. Since the night we met, my life has only gotten better. Thank you for all of your love and support, and most of all, thank you for being such a wonderful mother to our children.

~Andrew Fine

Introduction

Before every commercial airline flight, passengers receive a set of standardized FAA-mandated safety instructions. They're told how to fasten a seatbelt. They're told how to locate the closest emergency exit. They're also informed that in the case of sudden cabin depressurization, oxygen masks will fall automatically from the overhead compartments, and that parents traveling with small children should put their own masks on before attending to their little ones.

This last instruction is necessary because most parents are inclined to help their kids *before* they help themselves. It's just parental instinct. But how are you supposed to strap a mask over the face of a terrified, struggling 4-year-old when you're oxygen-deprived and probably on the verge of passing out?

Sometimes, the best way to take care of others is to take care of yourself first. Unfortunately, like a panicked parent who reflexively tries to provide life-saving oxygen to her child while her own brain shrivels from lack of oxygen, most of us have our priorities so out of whack we end up undercutting even our most well-intentioned efforts. When we fail, it's not because we're "lazy," "undisciplined," or "unfocused." Far from it. In fact, some of us are task-oriented to such an extreme we're blind to everything else around us, including the often-significant obstacles we're putting in our own way. This is why studies show "workaholics" are actually some of the most inefficient people in any professional environment.

I'll give you a personal example of this seemingly paradoxical phenomenon. I love my work, and for years I worked seven days a week. As my family's breadwinner, I believed such professional dedication was my duty as husband and father. I would go into the office early, skip lunches, work late. When I finally did come home, I'd say hello to my wife, gives my kids a quick hug, sometimes grab a bite from the fridge, then retreat to the bedroom and go right back to work. A few hours later, I'd give the kids their goodnight kisses, read them a bedtime story, and then again put my nose to the proverbial grindstone.

As you might imagine, this behavior didn't go over well with my family. In fact, my wife and kids were getting pretty bummed out. One day I overheard my son ask my wife, "How come Daddy's not spending time with us?" She told him what I thought was the truth: "Daddy is so busy, he can't get caught up."

My son considered this, then asked, "Can't they put him in a slower class?"

I had to laugh. Who wants to be put in a slower class? The point of business is to be successful by outperforming the competition and providing greater value to customers. If anything, I wanted to be put in the "gifted" class. I wanted to take on *more* work than anyone, and then deliver beyond all expectations. If I did this, I thought my bosses would respect me. I thought my colleagues would respect me. And, of course, I thought I would make more money. All of which I wanted. Desperately.

Achieving these goals, I reasoned, meant finishing everything on my to-do list as quickly as possible. So, I worked. And worked. And you know what happened? The harder I worked, the *behinder* I got. *So I worked even harder*. I came in on weekends. I was getting 100 emails a day. Some of them were important, but a lot of them weren't. The problem was distinguishing one from the other. I would have my to-do list, but eventually my list grew bigger than when I started.

At the same time, I would read about people like Elon Musk, the CEO of four companies, and wonder, how the hell can he do it? How can he complete his to-do lists? Speaking of which, do you make to-do lists? Most of us create them mentally, if not literally. Think about yours for a moment. Not just the one you've made for today or for this week, but *all* the to-do lists you've made in the past few months. How many times have you gotten through every item? If you answered, "each time," congratulations. Maybe you should write a book on time management!

Seriously, though, for us mere mortals, getting it *all* done is usually more a dream than a reality. And, for most of us, failing to reach our goals, however lofty, can make us feel guilty, discouraged, frustrated, and even depressed.

That's certainly how I felt at times. Even though I received four promotions in the span of just a few years, each one made me feel less secure than before. It's funny, but the more responsibility I acquired, the less in control I felt. I knew I couldn't go on like this. Something had to change. I looked for answers. I read a lot of books like *The 4-Hour Work Week* and *7 Habits of Highly Effective People*. I went to seminars and listened to "expert" speakers.

This all led to a startling revelation: I will *never* get everything done. And neither will you. Seriously. You'll never get it all done, no matter how many times you get up early, stay late, make to-do lists, and vigorously cross off tasks when they're complete. There will *always* be more jobs to do, more fires to extinguish, more problems to solve.

You're never going to read everything or get to every task. Because as you're working hard, grinding away, the assignments will keep piling up. The ancient Greeks had this figured out millennia ago when they wrote the myth of Hercules and the Hydra, a multiheaded monster. When one head was lopped off, two more would grow in its place. Even for a powerful demigod like Hercules, the harder he worked, the *behinder* he got.

Now, this isn't just my opinion or ancient Greek mythology. Robert Half

International (one of the United States' largest and oldest staffing companies) recently did a study and found the average, full-time manager in the United States is backed up with six months' worth of projects, assignments, and things to do. Did you get that? *Six months.* That's the bad news —

But here's the good news: There may never be enough time to get everything done, but there's always enough time to get the most important things, the *right* things, done. Robert Half says the average worker operates at a mere 50 percent capacity. Both managers and employees are capable of so much more. So how do we get closer to 100 percent and maintain a well-balanced, happy life?

Let me answer my own question with another question. Have you ever noticed your most productive day is the day before you go on vacation? This is because your instincts kick in to identify and complete the most important tasks: You whip through your emails, return phone calls, finish that project, and sign those expense reports, all before you get home in time to pack your luggage. Check the door locks. Call Uber. Grab your tickets. Arrive to the airport with ample time to get through security and find your gate. But, wait.

Are the garden weeds pulled? Has the dishwasher been emptied? Is your sock drawer properly arranged? Who cares? There's a plane to catch!

You have your priorities.

Now, what if you acted this way every single day? Imagine how productive you could be. This book will show you that you *can* change how you work so your life is a heck of a lot more productive, balanced, and fun. The key is to maximize your efficiency and work more *intentionally*. Using the tools provided here you will be able to lead a happier, more balanced, and guilt-free existence, both at home and at the office. And you can also pass on these tools to your employees so your company is more successful and healthy as a whole.

So how is this book different from all the other time-management books on Amazon? My co-author Michael and I have analyzed some of the greatest thinkers on time management, looked for common threads, and added our own experiences. We also applied the insights of the 20th and 21st century's most brilliant time-management experts to the most modern set of variables;

you won't find a more contemporary approach to personal efficiency.

The skills we'll teach you have helped people achieve 50 percent to 70 percent increases in productivity. Just imagine that figure applied to your professional situation. And this number is a deliberately conservative estimate based on my own experiences, those of co-workers, and reviews of past calendars and time logs. The advice you will read has also resulted in people having more fun, both at work and at home. Each chapter includes action steps you can implement immediately. Now, in the spirit of true time management, we are going to break down what we will cover so you will be primed for maximum efficiency.

In Chapter One, we'll introduce you to the secrets of obtaining and promoting work-life balance. This includes new ways to think about prioritizing tasks, a working definition of balance, my special work-life formula, an introduction to the concept of the personal mission statement, and the what, why, and how of keeping your team members happy on the job.

In Chapter Two, we'll talk about how to time-manage people. I'll give you some startling data on the backlog crisis in the U.S.

and some reasons why we *over*work, why that's a problem, how to identify and eliminate unimportant tasks, Stephen Covey's four quadrants, the Pareto Principle, and a look at a new study on achieving happiness.

In Chapter Three, we'll show you what happens when you infuse some structure and intentionality into your work life. We'll talk about primetime and downtime, managing interruptions, and offer concrete changes you can make to decrease work day interruptions. We'll look at different ways to rethink work-day organization and recommend some apps that can help you with this task.

Chapter Four is all about setting and achieving goals. We'll discuss why it's important to include personal aspirations with professional ones and offer ways to track your achievements throughout the year. We'll also look at how to cultivate employee buy-ins so all of your team members embrace the same agenda. We'll show you different organizational structures and explain how to select the one that will best suit your team to attain success. We'll review management skills that build power-packing teams, how to establish norms generating trust, and some management dos and don'ts. We'll also offer ways you can help your employees track goals and ideas for how to reward your employees to give you their best.

In Chapter Five, you will learn how to motivate your staff. We will explore both the top-down, or hierarchical structure, and the bottom-up, or egalitarian structure, as well as some models that have been effective in business environments. We'll review the Golden Rule and the Hawthorne studies. We'll analyze examples of employee surveillance/micromanagement to understand why these models consistently fail. We'll look at deadlines and how to keep your employees current with the knowledge emerging daily in the business world. We will unpack the difference between motivation and de-motivation, and how to create thriving relationships with your employees that keep them wanting to meet your company's goals.

Chapter Six concerns feedback and the fact people only like to hear good things. We'll begin by providing you with the elements of strategic feedback designed to elicit the most positive responses from your team. We'll reveal why your employees are your best investment, and how proper communication and training can enhance your ROI. We'll explore positive versus negative feedback, why timing is important, and how to keep feedback constructive even if it's critical. We will also share valuable tips on the when, where, and how to conduct those important conversations. Importantly, we will help you view each feedback meeting as part of a larger and ongoing process.

In Chapter Seven, we'll show you how to become a delegation Jedi. We'll review examples of people who did not embrace delegation and the consequences of their mistakes. We will investigate the reasons why many managers don't delegate—and why their reasons don't hold water. We will show you how to identify the right people to delegate to, how to choose what to delegate, and why delegation/decentralization is actually good for your team using specific case studies. We'll compare the differences between skillful and unskillful delegation and point out common delegation errors. Then, we'll teach you how to empower employees, prioritize delegated tasks, and create timelines and systems for follow-up.

In the Conclusion, we will share how using our techniques can transform work/life horror stories into happily-ever-after tales and provide a big-picture look at implementing the necessary changes today. We'll wrap up with FAQs from overworked people such as yourself. By the time you finish the book, you'll know how to:

Identify and focus on the most important items of your to-do list.

Eliminate (needless) distractions.

Perform at your best.

Inspire your people to be *their* best.

Are you ready for a happy and balanced life? Put on that oxygen mask and get ready to jump!

~Andrew Fine, 2019

Chapter One:
Yes, A Successful Work-Life Balance Is Possible

"You can't have everything you want, but you can have the things that really matter to you."
        ~Marissa Mayer, president and CEO of Yahoo!

Walking Life's Tightrope

"Work-life balance" is a popular buzzword, one of those trendy phrases everybody uses, everyone thinks they understand, but no one really knows how to precisely define. And even among those who believe they understand the concept, very few can successfully put the idea into practice.

Perhaps this metaphor will help. Imagine yourself as a tightrope walker moving slowly along a narrow cable stretched between two high poles. This visual suggests what the proper work-life balance might feel like. With each step, you must make dozens of micro-adjustments just to keep inching forward. It's a delicate situation. Pitch too far to one side or the other, and you risk tumbling to your death.

This is why balance is so important, and contrary to popular belief, it's not something we *achieve* and then walk away from. It's something we need to continually work on and is in a constant state of flux, just like that tightrope.

Balance is Everywhere

The natural world craves order. You've no doubt heard the term "ecological balance" in regard to the environment. This equilibrium ensures predators have enough prey to eat, prey don't deplete their habitat through overpopulation, and flora attains the right size for its water, sunlight, and temperature requirements. If, on the other hand, predators eat too much, if prey propagate too quickly, if native plant life overgrows, the entire habitat can collapse.

Likewise, the galaxies, stars, and planets hold their positions relative to each other thanks to gravitational balance. Owing to this equilibrium, heavenly bodies don't wreak cosmic chaos. The moon doesn't fly away from Earth, Earth doesn't collide into the sun, and the sun doesn't explode like a giant 4th of July firework. Dropping down to the personal level, a biological balancing act known by scientists as homeostasis keeps your body from becoming too hot or too cold, prevents you from getting too much or too little oxygen, and manages the rate of cell division. Should any of your systems fail, the results can be disastrous. For instance, uncontrollable cell division can lead to malignancies and, ultimately, death.

Balance is also essential to our psychological and emotional health. Most psychologists recognize six basic emotional states: happiness, sadness, fear, anger, surprise, and disgust. (For an entertaining depiction of these in action, see Pixar's 2015 Academy Award-winning animated feature *Inside Out.*) Most of these emotions are short-lived. Fear, anger, surprise, and disgust tend to be experienced in short, concentrated bursts, after which you settle back into one of two default states: happiness or sadness.

Where We Want to Be

Certainly, most of us prefer happiness as our ideal state. Its pursuit is even inscribed in our Constitution. Now, it's important to recognize that the pursuit of happiness promised to us in our nation's founding documents is no guarantee of bliss, but is actually an invocation to pursue it, however we define it.

To aid us in this quest, we have built numerous institutions —political, economic, and technological—to promote joy, all while minimizing negative emotional states. One of these institutions, the pharmaceutical industry, has become a multibillion-dollar behemoth predicated on this natural desire for contentment. Meanwhile, America's entertainment industry, including movies, television, music, and video games, is valued at about $720 billion, and is expected to surpass $1 trillion by 2025.

Still, in spite of the availability of so many distractions and prescription pick-me-ups, many individuals live in a perpetual state of sadness. No doubt you have met these people better known as pessimists, cynics, fatalists, and yes, even Debbie Downers. When the tilt toward sadness becomes too powerful, clinical depression can result. And this can lead to self-loathing, fatigue, catatonia, and even suicide.

If happiness is such a worthy and universal goal, how best should we pursue it?

Can Work Make Us Happy?

Many of us try to find happiness—and meaning—in our work. The notion of being "married to the job" is commonplace among workers, especially managers, executives, and professionals in most developed countries. (It's especially true since most of us spend more time with our co-workers than we do with our families.) And the higher one's position and compensation, the greater is the devotion one tends to have to their career. Today, simply working a conventional 40-

hour workweek is considered putting in the *minimum* at many companies. Want to get a raise or a promotion? The new reality is you'd better be prepared to work 50, 60 or even 80 hours per week.

As to be expected, chronic overtime can take its toll. According to workplace psychologist Jennifer Newman, working long hours can lead to not only fatigue, but also to injuries, psychological problems, and illnesses, such as heart and lung disease, arthritis, diabetes, and cancer. "These health effects are cumulative," she said in a March 2017 interview with CBS News. "A few long days won't do it. But, if long hours become a way of life, your health can suffer." Likewise, according to numerous studies, habitual overtime also can lead to burnout, which often means low productivity and low morale, deadly to business success.

What to Do About It

Now, I don't know about you, but all the money in the world won't help me if I've worked myself into an early grave. I want to be in good shape (mentally and physically) to enjoy my family, my off-time, even the work itself. To avoid the downside of overworking, it is now more crucial than ever to achieve a work-life balance. And this can only be achieved by taking small, consistent steps. *Persistently*.

In 1937, author Napoleon Hill published the now-classic motivational guide *Think and Grow Rich*. According to legend, Hill met and interviewed billionaire Andrew Carnegie, who introduced him to some of the most successful people in America at the time, including industrialist Henry Ford, inventor Thomas Edison, and retail marketing pioneer John Wanamaker, just to name a few.

During a 20-year period, Hill researched and examined the paths these and other top achievers took to achieve success. (Carnegie came to the United States as a penniless boy from Scotland; he believed that if he could achieve great success, everybody else could, too.) Carnegie tasked Hill with finding a new philosophy for success that any man on the street could apply to his own life and see positive results.

Carnegie wanted Hill to find the common thread between the world's most successful people and answer the question, "What did all these men do to make them successful and how can the average man apply this to his own life to become successful?" Hill's conclusion: Yes, some successful people are born rich, but most are not. Some are educated, but many are not.

Hill found many variables in his 20-year study of successful people, but he found one commonality they all shared: Hill called it having a "definite major purpose," which basically means the most successful people in the world climbed to great heights and achieved prosperity through simple goal setting, hard work, and perseverance. Basically, life's winners set big goals and just don't quit, ever. He applied this philosophy to his own work, and as a result created what became one of the most successful self-help books of all time (it took Hill 20 years to complete it, note the *perseverance* part of that formula!)

You Can Do It, Too

However, before ever setting foot on the path to Hill's idea of success and achievement, you must decide what happiness means to you. You have to determine for yourself what you value. In other words, you must prioritize. A good place to start is to consider psychologist Abraham Maslow's Hierarchy of Needs.

Maybe you learned about this concept in school or in a workshop. Maslow's paradigm contains a triangle divided into five horizontal layers, one atop the other. The bottom layer he labeled *Physiological* and includes basics such as food, water, health, and shelter. Next on the hierarchy is *Safety*, living free from all types of violence. The third and middle level pertains to *Love and Belonging*. Recognizing people are social creatures, Maslow pointed out we need connections with others. Second from the top, *Esteem*, signifies having a solid, positive sense of oneself. Finally, at the summit stands *Self-Actualization*. This refers to achieving one's goals, developing talents, and creating a good standing in society.

Maslow's hierarchy is pyramid-shaped because each level is fundamentally more important to existence than the ones above it. If you don't have access to life's basic necessities, such as food and shelter, it's unlikely you'll become a world-famous concert violinist. Likewise, if you reside in a war zone, chances are slim you're doing much speed dating. And if you live alone without the support of friends or family, you'll probably find little joy in even the grandest of mansions. Based on this pyramid, it is plain to see success in life is tied to prioritizing, satisfying more and more meaningful needs.

Self-Actualize Now

Now, I'm going to go out on a limb here and suggest most readers have successfully achieved the first two levels of Maslow's hierarchy. You probably have sufficient food and shelter, and you're (hopefully) in good health. You probably also don't live in constant fear for your life and property. Free from such concerns, you're focused on achieving the top two goals: Esteem and Self-Actualization.

But what about the level in the middle, Love and Belonging? Multiple studies reveal that, for most people, spending time with loved ones is key to attaining happiness. Without this piece in place, you'll be hard-pressed to achieve the higher desires on the triangle. What does this mean practically? It suggests you must find happiness in your relationships and your family life to ever hope to be successful in the categories of Esteem and Self-Actualization. In other words, you can't achieve your professional goals until you've achieved your personal ones.

Q.T.

Now, as anyone who has ever developed a meaningful relationship knows, interpersonal success requires time. So, let's talk about time. There's *quantity* of time and then there's *quality* of time. One way to think about work-life balance is Quality of Time at Work/Quantity of Time at Home. At the office, it's important that every hour invested produces some kind of measurable yield. At work, time is money. This is why many employees are paid by the clock and professionals bill by the hour. It's different at home where the benefits of time may be far less measurable—or predictable

Take time with your kids, for example. Those memorable moments that make parenting so special can't be predicted, let alone scheduled like a staff meeting or proposal deadline. Let's say you schedule a day to take your family to a local theme park. Everyone seems to be having fun until one of the kids throws a tantrum. Another drops her ice cream cone. The kids get overtired, cranky, maybe even nauseated. Well, that's $100-plus down the drain and you could have just gone to the park down the street for free! The next weekend, it's raining, and everyone stays home and pops popcorn and plays Monopoly. And everyone has a great time. Whodathunk it? The bottom line is that the *quantity* of time you spend with your family is important because the real good times—the memorable times—are unpredictable, and you need to give them plenty of time to arise spontaneously.

Of course, the same holds true with your spouse or significant other. You need to spend enough time with this individual to cultivate a meaningful relationship. How do you do this? Beyond sitting on the couch and staring into each other's eyes, it doesn't hurt to do the stuff you (presumably) did when you first got together: take vacations. Go on outings. Explore nature. Visit museums. Play board games. Make love.

Want to pursue happiness like the Constitution suggests? It's simple. The more time you spend at home, the more likely it is that life's special moments will happen while you're there. Even better, your work-life will benefit from increased time spent with the people you love. Sure, you can put in the occasional 60-hour work week, but mostly this kind of effort isn't sustainable long-term. Instead, a focus on quality will enable you to get more accomplished between 8 a.m. and 5 p.m. than you ever could through grinding it out. In addition, if you're grounded at home, you're likely to make fewer mistakes at work, be at your most creative, and miss fewer days due to illness or injury.

Don't Be a Jerk

Now that we realize the negative effects overwork can wreak on our body and psyche, we're apt to be more motivated to improve our work-life balance. Similarly, recognizing how imbalances lead to negative outcomes, we are more inclined to encourage our employees to strive for similar equilibrium. As managers, one of the key things we can do is to show our employees we care about their happiness, not just as workers, but as fellow people. So, how do you do communicate this type of caring?

The first rule is pretty simple: Don't be a jerk.

Did you ever have a boss you thought was a jerk? *Why* was he or she a jerk? Maybe they made you feel bad on the job or demeaned you in front of others. Maybe they made unreasonable requests or didn't care about your welfare. (Even having a boss roll his eyes at you can really hurt your feelings and stick with you for a long time. I know firsthand!) Whatever they did, at some point they lost your loyalty and became a "jerk."

Here's an example from my own experience with a jerky boss. After an abrupt personnel change, the boss I loved—who had hired me—left. She was replaced quickly by a guy we'll call Tony. When Tony and I met, I told him about a vacation I had planned and had cleared with the previous beloved manager.

When I mentioned this, he said, "Well that's nice, we'll see if you still get to go."

His dismissive attitude made me angry. Talk about getting off on the wrong foot. Money had already been spent. I had arranged travel plans and lodging with friends. They had arranged to take time off from their jobs. Based on this jerk's actions, my buddies stood to lose their vacations, too.

So, what did I do in the wake of this jerk's actions? I began looking for a new job. Luckily, I found one before the trip, which was only a month away, so I could say, "Sayonara, Tony!" (By the way, this conversation about my vacation was about as pleasant as any he and I ever had.) As you might imagine, Tony didn't care about his staff or their personal lives and made little effort to hide it. Other people had similar experiences with this guy. Clearly, that first impression stuck with me, because I'm still describing 15 years later.

Bottom-line: If you have the privilege to lead people, you have a responsibility to consider their welfare. It never helps to be dismissive about a quality-of-life issue affecting your staff. When you minimize the things others value, you risk losing their respect *and* their loyalty. As former President Theodore Roosevelt once said, "Nobody cares how much you know until they know how much you care." Want to get the best out of your people? Start by seeing them as people with their own hierarchy of needs. Respecting what makes them happy will lead to their trust and loyalty, leading to your own increased productivity—and happiness.

Happiness Goes Around (And Around)

Not being a jerk is just the beginning. In fact, it should be a low bar to attain. The reality is that it takes a lot more than not being a tyrant to keep your employees happy. Want to create happiness in the workplace? CEO and leadership coach Camille Preston, Ph.D., in her *Forbes* article, "Promoting

Employee Happiness Benefits Everyone," defines happiness as feeling like you matter, what you're doing is important, and that you're part of something that's progressing.

Similarly, Robert Half describes workplace happiness as a combination of enthusiasm, interest, contentment, empowerment, control, respect for colleagues, and pride/ownership in work. He also emphasizes that managers should strive for fairness and respect with their employees. They should reward intelligent risk-taking and show appreciation and support while avoiding micromanagement.

A New Paradigm

But hang on a second. Why is it so important that employees be happy? It's *work* after all. No one is happy at work, right? Just ask Dilbert. That's antiquated thinking. Many recent studies demonstrate happy workers are more productive than miserable ones. To this end, Gretchen Rubin, *The New York Times* bestselling author of *The Happiness Project*, states that happy personnel bring four major benefits to any workplace environment:

1. They are more productive.
2. They are better leaders.
3. They are more creative.
4. They are better team players.

In other words, happy employees allow companies to operate more efficiently. And that's good for any company's bottom line. Especially yours. Further to this point, in a February 2018 column in *Recruiter*, Stuart Hearn, CEO of Clear Review, explains that happy workers stick with you, giving you their best: "Happy employees—are loyal employees. If a person likes their office, enjoys their role, and is comfortable with their colleagues, they're less likely to leave. A happy workforce means lower turnover overall, which means you won't have to spend significant time and money looking for replacements who will probably also leave in due course."

So much for Tony's management style, right? But don't just take Hearn's word for it. Entrepreneur and business consultant Damon Burton agrees with this assessment. In a January 2018 column in *Talent and Management* HR, he wrote:

"Turnover is a huge loss of time in a variety of respects.

Wasted/lost time having trained the (now gone) employee

Time needed to post job listings to hire a replacement

Significant time interviewing replacement candidates

Once you finally find someone, you have to train that position all over again."

Happy employees, on the other hand, are more likely to stay at their jobs longer and minimize turnover expenses. One Social Market Foundation study cited by *Forbes* in December 2017 even found that happy employees are 20 percent more productive than unhappy ones, which leads to increasing profitability. Importantly, achieving such happiness need not be expensive. According to the results of one experiment, "Having spent approximately two dollars per person on drinks and snacks, productivity was boosted by almost 20 percent for a short period of concentrated work. This helped confirm that the result was not reliant on any particular type of happiness shock."

Make Happiness Your Workplace Reality

Hopefully, by now I've convinced you that taking steps toward making your employees happy is one of the smartest things you can do as a manager. But it's not always clear how to do this. The aforementioned Rubin provides some ideas in her research: Recognize employee successes; give them a sense of belonging; encourage them to have fun and form meaningful relationships; establish work-life boundaries and set a time for disconnecting from work; and inspire them to take care of themselves. Some innovative companies stage fitness challenges to encourage exercise. Along the same lines, why not introduce a Friday cocktail hour following a midday yoga class? Or bring in lunchtime speakers to educate employees about mindfulness or the importance of sleep, major factors in maintaining overall health.

Gifts are another way to create happy work lives for your employees. A study by the Martiz Institute and the Incentive Research Foundation concluded non-cash awards are powerful employee incentives. Referencing this study in a May 2018 column in *Inc.*, Firebrand Group founder and CEO Jeremy Goldman advises transparency between managers and employees to inspire trust, an essential element of a happy relationship with the boss. He also suggests planning fun outings for the team and providing opportunities for training and career development. These are concrete and simple ways to communicate to your team you care.

Now that you've seen how happiness is influenced by the ways you spend your day and the optimal way to obtain the best from your people is to honor the ways they spend their days, let's discover how to time-manage for maximum results. In the next chapter we will also learn how to determine what's important and what's not so important when it comes to achieving greater work/life balance.

Action Steps

Create a personal mission statement articulating, in the broadest possible terms, how you will achieve happiness. What does happiness look like to you? What values does it reflect? How is your goal likely to impact others? What kind of legacy will it create?

When writing your mission statement, keep it simple. A single sentence is ideal. Examples include: To leave my children a better world. To create more opportunities for today's youth. To inspire hope and love with every person I meet. Your mission statement is not set in stone and can change over time but it should serve as your inspiration and lodestar every day.

Make a list of three to five personal long-terms goals you believe will make you happy. These can include things like fall in love and marry, start my own company, save enough money for retirement. Be as specific as possible. If you want to start your own business, what kind of company do you want to start? If you want to save enough money for retirement, how much money will that be? When selecting your goals, consider both your personal mission statement and Maslow's Hierarchy of Needs. Confirm you have fulfilled the lower tiers before aiming for anything higher.

Make a list of three to five short-term goals you need to achieve each of the long-term goals you listed. For example, what steps can you take to fall in love and marry, begin your own company or save enough money for retirement? Again, be as specific as possible.

Create a realistic schedule for accomplishing each of the steps you outlined in Steps 2 and 3. Track your progress, refer to this schedule daily and hold yourself accountable. Studies show that fewer than 5 percent of adults have written goals they regularly follow up on, so this exercise alone will set you apart from everyone else.

Chapter Two:
Manage Time, Manage People, Manage Life

"I defeated Austria because they did not know the value of 5 minutes."
~Napoleon Bonaparte

They're Not Making Any More of It

We all know time is valuable. But what makes time uniquely prized is it's our one *truly* unrenewable resource. Like gold, time is finite. But gold, unlike time, is malleable. It can be pounded into thin sheets or melted down and cast into an infinite number of shapes. Time, on the other hand, is immutable—unchanging. Contrary to the premise of the *Back to the Future* franchise, time cannot be reshaped or altered in any way. (At least not yet. Although if you think about it, if someone did eventually invent a time machine, they could go back to our present and tell us all about it. Okay. Enough about time machines.)

Returning to our gold analogy, while there may be vast untapped resources of gold in the seas and in outer space, we could explore the cosmos and never find additional reserves of time. Time is also unrecyclable. Once it's used, it cannot be reused. It's gone forever. In this sense, time is like petroleum, another valuable, finite, and unrenewable resource upon which our modern civilization depends. But there are alternatives to petroleum. As an energy source, oil can be replaced by solar power, wind power, hydroelectric power, geothermal power, fuel cells, and nuclear fission. Petroleum also has synthetic substitutes. Not so with time. Time cannot be manufactured in a lab. There are no *alternative* forms of time. The time we have is all the time we're ever going to get, and we're losing it second by second at the same steady, unstoppable rate, even as you read the words on this page.

All of which is to say managing time is really, really important. And not just your time, but the time of any people for whom you are responsible. As a company CEO, top executive, middle manager, or team leader, your ability to use time properly will have a direct impact on your company's success, and by extension, your own career track.

People Are Not Machines

Note that I did *not* say your goal as a manger should be to squeeze as much productivity as you can out of every labor-hour. People are not machines whose output can be measured on a minute-by-minute basis. We are multifaceted, highly sophisticated beings. As James D. Watson, co-discoverer of the structure of DNA once said, "The brain is the most complex thing we have yet discovered in our universe." As a result of our brains and our brawn, human productivity is subject to a wide range of variables, including, but not limited to, mood swings, circadian rhythms, chemical stimulants, personal motivations, social pressure, sleep deprivation, and yes, even simple boredom.

At first glance, the existence of so many peccadilloes might seem to make a strong case for replacing most workers with intelligent machines as quickly as the technology allows. But remember, it's these same imperfections that give rise to the uniquely human qualities of originality, creativity, ingenuity, and genius. All of which are things you want to maximize as a good leader.

Unfortunately, as noted in the previous chapter, most businesspeople manage time with all the subtlety of a pneumatic jackhammer. They believe the only way to deal with the tyranny of time is through the application of brute force. Work longer hours and achieve greater results, the thinking goes. Or, as we are told repeatedly from childhood, the only way to achieve success is through long hours and great personal sacrifice. Because of this wrongheaded thinking, Americans are some of the most overworked people in the Western world.

America, the Overworked

In a 2016 report by the Organization for Economic Cooperation and Development

(OECD), the United States came in 13th among the group's 35-member nations in terms of hours worked annually. According to the OECD's report, the average American put in 1,789 hours per year. While this ranking may not appear particularly alarming, it's important to note we were mostly outranked by second-tier economies, such as Mexico (#1 @2,250 hours/year), Russia (#5 @1,974 hours/year), and Estonia (#11 @1,855 hours/year).

Although the U.S. economy is by far the largest in the OECD, it seems our workers are virtual wage-slaves when compared to most other advanced economies, including Japan (#17 @1,742 hours/year), Canada (#20 @1,703 hours/year), the U.K. (#23 @1,676 hours/year), and France (#31 @1,472 hours/year). And those industrious Germans, famous for their ceaseless productivity? They're at the bottom of the list with a per-worker average of just 1,288 hours per year. "Okay, fine," you may be thinking, "all those extra hours must surely yield big dividends, right?"

Actually, for all of our efforts, we Americans get little in return compared with the rest of the developed world. For one thing, we are the only Western democracy with no federally mandated cap on weekly working hours. Also, although workers in our country's rapidly shrinking unionized labor force receive overtime pay for labor in excess of 40 hours per week, non-unionized hourly workers, salaried workers, and, of course, the self-employed (about 10 percent of the total workforce) receive no such benefits.

America is also the only major industrialized country with no federally mandated maternal or parental leave time, nor federally mandated vacation time. Sweden, for example, guarantees 46 days of paid maternity/parental leave, 25 paid vacation days, plus 16 paid national holidays per year. French workers receive 45.5 days of paid maternity/parental leave, a minimum of 30 paid vacation days, plus eight paid holidays annually. And the Germans? Fifty days of paid maternity/parental leave, 24 paid vacation days, and 10 paid holidays. Even tiny Croatia guarantees its citizens 28 to 45 days of paid maternity leave, 20 paid vacation days, and 13 paid holidays. America? Zero, zero and eight.

Vacation? No Thanks. I'm Good Here at My Desk

Even when Americans receive paid vacation through their employers, few actually take advantage of the time they are given. According to a May 2018 report from the organization Project: Time Off, 52 percent of employees who earned vacation time in 2017 did not take the maximum time allowed. This added up to 705 million unused vacation days, up from 662 million the year before. These 705 million unused days not only result in additional wear and tear on the average worker's psyche, but also represent a $255 billion opportunity the American economy is not capturing. Project: Time Off researchers claim this time, if used, could have generated 1.9 million jobs in the recreation and hospitality sectors.

Another disturbing trend the Project: Time Off report identified was the rising popularity of so-called "workcations." Workcations, now taken by approximately 10 percent of workers, are trips in which busy people schedule specified chunks of time to work remotely. In other words, while a business executive might take two weeks off to fly her family to Florence, she might still dedicate three or four hours each day to work from her hotel while her family tours the Duomo.

The benefit of workcations is that, in many cases, workers can visit destinations without being charged against their vacation time for doing so. It also keeps them in the loop, so there's less frantic catching up to do upon their return. Of course, the downside to working vacations is that many of the emotional, psychological, and spiritual benefits vacations are intended to impart—specifically, the chance to unwind, recharge, and just chill—are significantly diminished.

Overwork = Less Productivity

Why is overwork such a big problem? If you're reading this book, chances are you at least know what it's doing to you. But did you know that, in fact, working more hours doesn't lead to more productivity? In a 2015 study conducted by Erin Reid, a professor at Boston University's Questrom School of

Business, managers at a large international business consulting firm were asked to evaluate the performance of a large group of their employees without knowing the number of hours the individual employees actually logged.

Although consultants at this firm were expected to put in long hours, work evenings, and sacrifice weekends, many found ways to cut corners and look busier than they actually were. As it turned out, the lowest producers appeared to put in more hours than the actual A-Players. Interestingly, researchers at California's Stanford University have actually developed a formula expressing the relationship between hours worked and productivity gained/lost:

$$60 \times P_{60} < 40 \times P_{40}$$

In this formula, P_{60} is the average productivity of employees working 60-hour weeks, and P_{40} is the average productivity of employees working 40-hour weeks. The formula reveals productivity during 60-hour weeks is less than two-thirds of that delivered in typical 40-hour work weeks. And we're not just talking about productivity dropping during the extra 20 hours put in weekly, but during *each hour across the board.*

Overwork is Also Bad for Your Health

More bad news on the overworking front. Companies in which employees habitually overwork—be it the result of mandated overtime or just a competitive corporate culture—tend to suffer from high rates of absenteeism, employee turnover, on-the-job accidents, production/operational errors and, in the most extreme situations, workplace violence.

It is not hard to see why overworking leads to such negative effects. Employees who work long hours, either voluntarily or otherwise, tend to suffer from insomnia, memory loss, communication issues, and substance abuse, not to mention increased rates of obesity, high blood pressure, depression, and diabetes. A 2015 study from University College London reviewed heart attack risk in 600,000 workers and stroke risk in more than 500,000 workers. The study focused on the link between these potentially life-ending events and work hours, compensating for such factors as smoking, alcohol consumption, physical activity, and even pre-existing medical conditions, including high blood pressure, diabetes, and high cholesterol.

Their conclusion: People who work more than 55 hours per week have a 13 percent greater risk of heart attack and were 33 percent more likely to suffer a stroke compared with people who worked 35- and 40-hour work weeks. In other words, working too many hours really can put you in an early grave.

The Cult of the Overachiever

So why *do* we overwork when we know it's so bad for us? According to a May 2013 article written by Joan C. Williams for the *Harvard Business Review*, the answer is simple: pride, status, and simple old-fashioned machismo. "Work devotion marries moral purity with elite status," Williams wrote. "Way back when I was a visiting professor at Harvard Law School, I used to call it the cult of business smartness. How do the elite signal to each other how important they are? 'I am slammed,' is the socially acceptable way of saying 'I am important.' Fifty years ago, Americans signaled class by displaying their leisure; think banker's hours (9 a.m.-3 p.m.)." Today's elite—journalist Chrystia Freeland calls them "the working rich"—display their extremely full schedules.

Likewise, a 1999 study of lawyers by Cynthia Fuchs Epstein, sociologist and emeritus distinguished professor of sociology at the Graduate Center of the City University of New York, demonstrates putting in exorbitant working hours is seen as a "heroic activity," a way to demonstrate one is a *real man*. "There's a kind of machismo culture that you don't sleep," one father tells her, concluding, "The successful enactment of this masculinity involves displaying one's exhaustion, physically and verbally, in order to convey the depth of one's commitment, stamina, and virility."

A hundred years ago, inventor Thomas Edison used to famously boast he was able to regularly produce works of genius on only four hours of sleep per night. In fact, he was regularly caught taking catnaps at work to recharge his mental batteries. More recently, entrepreneur Elon Musk has made similar claims, only to be found sleeping in the corner of his office or in work areas where employees have to literally step over his prostrate form. Yes, there *are* people who can functional well on limited sleep, but they are truly few and far between.

To many workers, especially younger men and women at the bottom of the professional hierarchy, there is the fear, sometimes stated, sometimes implicit, that taking time off proves to employers you're easily replaceable, if not wholly disposable. In an era when companies are actively downsizing and looking for any excuse to cut personnel, you don't want to give your manager the opportunity to see how easy it is to get along without you, the thinking goes.

Fighting Off Backlog

What tends to get lost when overworking is the pursuit of happiness. Sure, there are folks who are happiest when they are at work; who eat, breathe, and sleep their jobs. These individuals are merriest working every minute of their waking day. But that's not most people. An 80-year study conducted by Harvard University on happiness concluded being happy means prioritizing three things:

Close relationships, especially marriage

Taking care of oneself physically, emotionally, and financially

Being intentional—actively choosing to be happy.

(You'll notice winning the prize for working the most hours was not on the list.) These Harvard researchers also discovered something else interesting: Deep feelings of loneliness tend to be a predictor of health problems to the same degree as alcoholism, smoking, and poor genetics. It is worth noting that by *loneliness*, they didn't mean simply being alone. According to the research, one's relationships tend to be positive only when true intimacy is present. Bottom line: Living to work and developing no serious relationships can be detrimental to your health.

The 4 Quadrants

To reduce unnecessary overworking, to free up our time to develop relationships that bring true value to our lives, the time we do spend working needs to be just that—*working*. It needs to be productive, free of procrastination, and focused on our most important tasks. Priorities need to be clear so we can get important things done and move on. High priorities always need to be separated from low priorities, so we must first identify unimportant tasks and eliminate them. There's nobody better to help us with this than Stephen Covey, bestselling author of *The 7 Habits of Highly Effective People.*

In his book, Covey divides the traditional to-do list into four quadrants. Each quadrant is delineated by level of importance and urgency. Comparing how your activities match up with Covey's target percentages will help you see where you should focus your nonrenewable time—and what's standing in your way of being time effective.

Let's now break down the quadrants, one by one.

Quadrant #1: Urgent and Important

Quadrant #1 designates items as crisis level of importance. Urgent and important, these are tasks simply have to get done NOW NOW NOW! Examples include finishing a report due at 8 a.m. tomorrow to your boss that will determine if you have still hold a job, responding to a medical emergency, or catching a flight. Other contenders could be paying overdue rent or responding to a very important—and very angry—client by phone.

By their nature, you might think crises are things that cannot be predicted or avoided. After all, no one plans to have a heart attack, get a flat tire, or deal with an overflowing toilet. But the fact is, most crises are manufactured. They result from poor planning, procrastination, and not paying attention.

Did you forget your report is due to your boss by tomorrow morning? Maybe you should invest in a day planner or take advantage of the Reminder app on your smartphone. Are you scrambling to pay your rent 15 days into the month? You probably should have paid the rent on the first. Rushing to catch that airline flight? Perhaps you should have left 30 minutes earlier. With the right amount of careful planning and foresight, responding to crises can be confined to as little as 5 percent of your average work day. Ironically, we tend to think our promotions and raises come from the work we do in Quadrant #1, but they actually come from the work we do in Quadrant #2

Quadrant #2: Not Urgent, Important

Quadrant #2 pertains to quality/effectiveness, or tasks that are not urgent but are nonetheless important. These might include planning, goal setting, training, normal work assignments, school projects, picking up the dry cleaning, or grocery shopping. They can also include physical exercise and time spent with your family. Items on this list are important not because of any immediate life-or-death, sink-or-swim, win-or-lose direness, but because they pose long-term consequences if not completed.

If you habitually fail to complete work assignments, you'll likely be fired. If you fail to exercise, you'll probably start gaining weight and your health will suffer. Don't go grocery shopping for long enough and you'll wake up to an empty refrigerator. (Think of the term paper you had to do for school—it was important, but not urgent, so you procrastinated until it gradually moved from Quadrant #2 to Quadrant #1.)

The fact is, because these important-but-not-urgent tasks lack immediate consequences and are easily procrastinated on, we tend to put them off—until they slide into Quadrant #1's danger zone. To avoid turning routine tasks into crisis-level headaches, try to make these tasks the focus of your day. Apportioning at least 75 percent of your working time to these items can be a helpful target. Prioritize these items and you'll be well on your way to living a happier, more fulfilling life.

Quadrant #3: Urgent, Not Important

Quadrant #3 refers to distraction/delusion. These are tasks that seem urgent but are not actually important. Examples include (low priority) emails and phone calls, co-workers' spontaneous visits, lengthy social lunches, people asking for favors, and most company meetings. In other words, Quadrant #3 is reserved for typical interruptions. Beware of Quadrant #3. It is important to manage these kinds of events; if left unchecked, they can hijack your day. Your boss occasionally will put you into Quadrant #3 on an assignment that she doesn't want to do or doesn't have time to do. The key to managing Quadrant #3 is this: Don't let anyone but YOUR BOSS put you into Quadrant #3. Target time allotment for these tasks should occupy no more than 15 percent.

Quadrant #4: Not Urgent, Not Important

Finally, we come to Quadrant #4 or waste. These are things that are not urgent *and* not important. Tasks such as these don't contribute to your life or your business. We know these well. These activities can *seem* important. They can even be fun and relaxing, but they won't bring you closer to your goals. Worse, they can also end up being a huge time suck. Examples include: long lunches, coffee breaks, gossiping with colleagues, and updating your Facebook status.

A related 2016 study by TeamLease World of Work Report found American workers now spend an average 2.35 hours of each work day on social media, leading to a 15 percent reduction in workplace productivity. Breaking the habit to check and post on your feed can be difficult, but in order to maximize your efficiency, you must. And you must encourage your subordinates to do the same. Try to restrict activities in this quadrant to no more than 5 percent of your working day but make a strong effort to eliminate them wherever and whenever you can. More time wasted *at* work equals less time away from work in which you could be doing other things of value and purpose

The Pareto Principle

As we think about putting tasks into quadrants, it's useful to consider the story of Vilfredo Pareto, economist and sociologist. This Italian scholar studied the intersection of politics and philosophy in the 1800s and used mathematics to better understand economic and social phenomena. In 1906, he developed what is known as the Pareto Principle (commonly known as the 80/20 rule) to describe his country's uneven distribution of wealth, claiming just 20 percent of the population generated up to 80 percent of it.

In time, Pareto's Principle was expanded to describe all economic activity worldwide once Pareto realized he could apply his theory to almost anything. For example, he noticed that 20 percent of people own 80 percent of the land. In Pareto's business activities he found 20 percent of activities accounted for 80 percent of his results. And 20 percent of his customers led to 80 percent of sales.

The Pareto Principle can also apply to you on an individual level when contemplating your daily schedule. Look at your email inbox for example. Twenty percent of emails and voicemails are probably important, 80 percent are not and can be deleted without being read (which will save you a lot of time). The top 20 percent of the tasks on a typical to-do list are more valuable than the bottom 80 percent of tasks.

The key to increasing your productivity is to continually focus on your top 20 percent and ignore, delegate, or eliminate your bottom

20 percent. As you chip away at that top 20 percent, more tasks will rise from the bottom 80 percent into your top 20 percent. Use Covey's quadrants to help identify your top 20 percent and remember this important rule: Never work on a task in your bottom 80 percent if you have a task in your top 20 percent that is undone. The better you understand how you should be using your nonrenewable time, the more productive— and happier you shall be.

Now that we have established a clear need and purpose for time management, the next chapter will offer specific steps you can take now to make the most from each hour of your working day.

Action Steps:

Tune in, turn on, drop out. Do you like staying on top of current events, reading the newspaper, and/or checking news feeds? If you want to create more time for work *and* play, take a 30-day hiatus from the news. Watch how you miss absolutely nothing important. Most people have a hard time with this suggestion, but it's liberating. If something important happens in the world, I promise someone else will tell you. Let your friends, family, and co-workers sift through all the unimportant news of the day, waiting to see or hear something that matters. By choosing to ignore it, you will create extra time for everything else in your life that I'm guessing is more important—*much* more important.

Create a time-tracker notebook. There is a famous adage in business that says, "If you can't measure it, you can't manage it." To manage your time, you're going to have to measure it. And that means keeping careful track of each working minute and how you spend it. How much time are you actually *working* while you are at work? Purchase a small notebook with lined paper. For each day, break each hour into 10-minute increments. This means for the typical nine-hour work day (including lunch), you should have 54-line entries. Every 10 minutes, log how you spent your time, assigning each activity to one of the four quadrants detailed earlier in this chapter: #1 Crisis, #2 Quality/Effectiveness, #3 Distraction/Delusion, or #4 Waste. Be brutally honest on how you judge your time. At the end of the day, if you see an hour or more devoted to #4, you'll see how serious your situation is and be more apt to make the necessary changes to save your most precious (and nonrenewable) resource. Are you spending too much time in Quadrant #4? Eliminate those habits immediately and you will see instant, positive results.

Track your interruptions for one week. How much time are you really spending in Quadrant #3? Most people underestimate this. Are you frequently interrupted? Who/what keeps interrupting you? Track those interruptions that *appear* to be urgent and start creating systems to eliminate them. Is it your email alerts? Turn them off. Is it your phone? Send it to voicemail. Your office neighbor? Don't be afraid to shut the blinds or office door once in a while. Little by little these small changes will add up to extra hours of productivity and keep you on track, moving quickly toward your most important goals. We'll discuss more ways to reduce interruptions and get you out of Quadrant #3 in the next chapter.

Chapter Three:
The Structure for Success

"The only place success comes before work is in the dictionary."
~Vince Lombardi, Hall of Fame
Football Coach

In our last chapter, we discussed the importance of managing time, how time is used, how time is wasted; and how greater productivity—and happiness—may be achieved not by investing more time in work, but by using smaller amounts of time more efficiently. In this chapter we're going to look at specific ways to achieve these efficiencies and provide you with tools to make the most out of every day.

The Importance of Structure

In discussing time management, we're going to talk a lot about structure. But what is structure and why is it so important to building a successful professional and personal life? When you hear the word "structure," you might picture a building under construction. That's an apt representation. Every building begins with a foundation upon which is built a framework, over which is laid a façade, and within which are added all manner of interior spaces and details.

Without a solid foundation in place, anything built above will eventually sag and collapse. Likewise, any accompanying framework not only needs to be solidly built, but also well thought-out. All of the components must be integrated to withstand stresses placed upon it. We've all seen buildings renovated over the years. Façades are torn down and updated. Interior spaces are reconfigured and remodeled. Roofs are removed and replaced. But the building's basic structure remains. In fact, if a building's structure is sound—if it has "good bones" to use the real estate vernacular—it can endure for a long time. Europe's centuries-old buildings offer this proof.

But structural importance extends well beyond architecture. In chemistry, for example, an atom's structure—the number of protons and neutrons in its nucleus, and the number of electrons orbiting it—determine the atom's weight, stability (radioactivity), and its properties. At room temperature, is the element a gas, a liquid or a solid? Can it easily combine with other elements? It all depends on the atom's structure. Structure is even more critical at the molecular level. The way atoms are arranged relative to one another can instill the resulting particle with all manner of qualities. From spectacular natural crystals to space-age alloys to the DNA carrying the instructions of life itself, it's all about structure.

Even something as seemingly intuitive as the arts is highly dependent on structure. Music, for example, is composed of a series of rigid and mathematically precise units of beats, measures, phrases, and movements. Movies also tend to follow a highly formalized three-act structure, with Act One (exposition/inciting incident) accounting for

25 percent of a film's running time, Act Two (development/obstacles) accounting for 50 percent, and Act Three (final battle/crisis/resolution) accounting for the final 25 percent. Any deviation from this structure tends to result in a film that seems slow, rushed, or otherwise off balance. Even fine art in general tends to be highly structured, the elements of composition— including focal points, perspective, color, movement, patterns, shapes, and, yes, rhythms—having been established and refined by experts over the centuries.

Knowing just how structure is required for balance, order, and yes, even beauty, let's consider how your time is structured and what we can do to create a daily structure that will stand the test of—well, time.

What a Way to Make a Living—

The average American workday begins at 8 a.m. and ends at 5 p.m. During this time, eight hours are allocated for work with one hour, usually noon to 1p.m., taken off for lunch. This structure may seem so entrenched in our national consciousness it feels like some authority on high mandated we schedule life this way. However, there is no holy reason for this structure. Nowhere is it codified in the Bible or any other sacred document that people must toil according to this schedule. It's just a construct society established to regulate workers' comings and goings.

Actually, the 8-to-5 schedule is a modern invention. Created in the early 20th century, it was generated to facilitate the growing industrial nature of our economy. Back when America was still an agricultural nation, most people's workday began around sunrise (even earlier if you were a dairy farmer) and ended at sundown. In late spring through early autumn, workdays could last 14 hours or more (depending on latitude).

Conversely, in winter, when days were shorter, and the ground frozen, only a few odd hours each day might be devoted to chores or routine property maintenance. It was only when manufacturing began supplanting agriculture that the traditional workday structure developed. Why? Burgeoning factories required all participants on hand when the assembly lines began to move. Also, back then, it was not unusual for shifts to run 12 hours or longer. Only in the 1930s, when labor unions became powerful, did our common 8-to-5 or 9-to-5 schedule go into effect.

Of course, common does not mean universal. Today, some utility plants and manufacturing facilities run three shifts a day, starting well before dawn and others commencing when most people are going to bed (known as the graveyard shift). Anyone working in a hospital, fire station, police department, or 24-hour grocery store is all too familiar with the rigors of a round-the-clock schedule. And while farmworkers' hours are still tied to seasonal time fluctuations, it has become common for many salaried professionals to put in hours going well into the night.

Despite such cultural constructs—and the structure American society has evolved to apportion our workdays—a major problem lurks. A fly in time management's ointment. The thing is, while a rigid schedule, be it 8 a.m. to 5 p.m. or 4 p.m. to midnight, might be right for your company, it may not be right for *you*. In spite of our culture's insistence that everyone get on the same workday page, each of us possesses a unique circadian rhythm determining when our performance peaks and ebbs. Let's call these periods primetime and downtime.

Primetime vs. Downtime

Primetime is the time of day when you're at your best. You feel energetic. Your senses are sharp, your reflexes quick. You're able to concentrate and focus for extended periods. Primetime is also conducive to entering *the zone*, the ideal creative flow state when time itself seems to melt away, allowing you to focus purely on the task at hand.

On the flip side, downtime is that time of day when your energy is low, when you feel sluggish and definitely not at your best. You have difficulty concentrating and are easily bored or distracted during these hours. Time slows to a crawl and you find yourself looking at the clock. Though some people like to joke that their downtime occurs between 8 a.m. to 5 p.m., according to researchers, about 25 percent of the population experience their prime in the morning. These early birds awake energized, ready to rock and roll. They tend to be at their peak around 9 or 10 o'clock; their energy waning as lunch approaches. In the afternoon, they tend to be sluggish, having long ago expended their excess energy. If they're lucky, they can make it to 9 p.m. before falling asleep in front of the television.

Another 25 percent of the population constitute the night owls. These folks tend to a have a hard time waking up. They're slow and have low energy levels throughout the day. Only when the sun goes down do they truly come alive, often performing at their peak until the wee hours of the morning. The remaining 50 percent of people are something between the early bird and the night owl. Usually requiring a cup or two of coffee to wake up, these in-betweeners can enjoy a few hours of peak productivity in the late morning, may become sluggish after lunch, then have another short burst of energy in the midafternoon before again tapering off for the evening.

Whether you are an early bird, a night owl, or an in-betweener has a lot to do with your genes and constitution. There's little anyone can do to make an early bird party past midnight or a night owl hit the gym at 6 a.m. before heading to the office. Instead, what you *can* do is recognize your personality type and structure your workday accordingly.

If You're an Early Bird—your mornings are primetime. Use these early hours to attend to your most important tasks, those of highest priority or that demand difficult, complex decision-making. In the afternoon, when your energy wanes, turn to your less demanding tasks, such as responding to emails, routine meetings, system-imposed activities, and daily administrative and cleanup activities.

If You're a Night Owl—start your day with the easy stuff: Emails. Administration. Staff meetings. As the day progressives, allot more time for important tasks and concentration-heavy assignments. If you have any flexibility, you might even structure your day so you arrive *late*—say, at 10 a.m.—but stay until 6 or 7 p.m., so you can take best advantage of your body's peak energy.

The important thing here is not *when* your primetime is, but that you *protect* your primetime. We can be two to three times more productive during our primetime, so do everything you can to control it and protect it from interruption. For example: block it out on your calendar, shut your office door, ignore electronic communications, and don't schedule regular, routine meetings during this time. Explain to your boss when your primetime is and that you would like to protect it whenever you can. (Your boss may have a different primetime and might have given little thought to when yours is.) It wouldn't hurt to know when your boss' primetime is too! The hours when you are at your peak will be your most productive, so get the most out of them every day.

Quick Action Steps: Role Playing

Stop reading now and figure out when your primetime is (if you haven't done so already).

Pledge to protect your primetime like you are a secret service agent and your primetime is the president of the United States (those guys take things seriously!).

Take the top 20 percent of your to-do list tasks and try to schedule them during your primetime. Marry them together and like a good Disney movie, you will all live happily ever after together. Repeat Step 3 as often as possible.

Stop Me If You've Heard This One

According to workplace researchers, the average office worker is interrupted 100 times a day. These interruptions include everything from phone calls, email alerts, requests from supervisors, and just chit-chatting co-workers. Working at home can provide some relief, but these environments can also provide plenty more distractions of their own, including spouses, kids, pets, neighbors, landscapers, solicitors—not to mention the ever-present temptation to check the Internet, fix that leaky faucet, grab a snack from the kitchen, or play a videogame.

Whether at home or work, interruptions can wreak havoc on productivity. According to a recent study by researchers at the University of California, Irvine, it takes about 23 minutes to recover from an interruption and put your brain fully back in gear. And with the average worker switching tasks every three minutes, according to the same UCI study, it's a miracle any work gets done at all. Ultimately, there are two solutions to control and minimize interruptions:

1. Try to reduce the total number of interruptions

2. Try to reduce the average length of each interruption

If you are the victim of frequent interruptions, there may be structural reasons for this—reasons you can change. Some of these strategies may seem a little extreme, but remember, *you* are the one with too much to do and too little time. Ask yourself, are those typical interruptions in your top 20 percent of things to do? Probably not. Here are some examples of classic offenders and instructions on how to combat them.

The High Traffic Lane

Do you have a work station, desk, or office close to a busy office traffic zone? Do co-workers or visitors constantly invade your personal space? Even a casual "Hi!" or "Good morning!" can generate an unwanted interruption, breaking your concentration and sapping your creative flow. If possible, find a more isolated work area less prone to sudden invasion.

The Eye of Sauron

But what if you can't move your workspace? That can still be okay as long as you re-orient your position so you're not as apt to make eye contact with passersby. Just the act of locking eyes for a moment can break your concentration. Taking steps to avoid this can prove beneficial even if it earns you the reputation of being anti-social.

The Candy Man

Do you have a candy jar on your desk or in your office? If you do, you might be popular with snackers who like to drop in for a quick handful of M&M's, but it won't do you any favors when it comes to increasing productivity. In fact, being the company snack depository practically invites interruptions. Get rid of the goodies. If you must have snacks on hand, keep them in a desk drawer away from public sight. Or put that candy dish in a break room or a lunch area, away from your desk. Even better, give it as a gift to your least-favorite co-worker.

The Host(ess) with the Most(ess)

Do you have an office with a comfy, overstuffed chair or two ready to accept guests? Again, this is another open invitation for people to interrupt you. If you must accommodate visitors on occasion, set a folding chair or two against the wall, or a high-backed bistro-style chair that is less than comfortable and conducive to hanging out. Your co-workers may think this is funny, but they'll also likely get the message.

Your Place or Mine?

When scheduling meetings, always coordinate the event in a separate meeting room or in a co-worker's space, never in your own. This is to avoid visitors showing up early and breaking your concentration. It also prevents people from staying longer than necessary. If you meet outside your workspace, you're free to arrive and leave at times most convenient for *you*.

The Drop-In

How do you deal with people who appear unexpectedly and ask, "Got a minute?" If you immediately drop what you're doing to give your visitor your undivided attention, you're doing yourself a disservice. Instead, prevent a short interruption from becoming a big one by saying something like, "I'll be free in an hour," or "I'll come by your place when I'm done here."

You could also try saying, "I've got just a couple of minutes." It's not rude, it's politely assertive. It doesn't really put a time limit on the conversation, but it lets them know you need them to get to the point. Or you could say, "no" plus an option – "I'm sorry, I can't right now but can you come back at 4:45? If it's unimportant, they will be wrapping up their work day at 4:45 and probably won't come back. If it is important and you need more time with them, make sure to reschedule for the following day. Remember: Don't feel guilty about zealously guarding your precious time.

The Happy Camper

Do you ever have people camp out in your office? They sit down, take a deep breath, and you can tell they aren't going anywhere for a long time. With your comfy, overstuffed chairs and your candy dish, it's no wonder they refuse to leave. You must take charge of the situation and stand up for yourself. Literally. Stand up. Begin to stroll. Even say, "Walk with me, I have to go to the bathroom." Make sure to invite them along, they will walk with you for a little while, get to the point quickly, and break away before you go into the bathroom.

The Chatterbox

Do you run into people who constantly trap you in a conversation and just won't stop talking? As always, you need to ease yourself out of the situation without coming off like a jerk. The first thing to do is break eye contact. If that doesn't work, offer a work-related reason like, "Sorry, I'm on a deadline" or "I have to prepare for a meeting." Be careful to avoid excuses that can be easily exposed, like, "I have to get to a meeting" when you might be found at your desk five minutes later. Always be polite; you don't want to hurt anyone's feelings, but if you have to run, be honest. Say, "Great speaking with you, I'm sorry but I do have to run —" Leave the conversation on a high note.

Graham Bell's Revenge

There are few things more jarring—or insistent—than a ringing phone. And once you're engaged in a phone conversation, ending it elegantly can prove extremely difficult. One way to keep phone calls at bay is to screen them. Simply send everything to voice mail. Some systems allow you to listen to messages as they are being recorded and pick up if it's something important or return it to later when you have more time.

You've Got Mail!

Back in ye olde tymes—before the invention of email—say, the 1980s—intra-office communications were quite different. They consisted of memos that had to be typed, duplicated, and manually distributed to the designated participants. As anyone who lived through these dark ages will attest, it was a long, labor-intensive, *expensive* process inhibiting people from issuing non-essential communications. (Although even then office workers complained about being buried under reams of memoranda about topics ranging from critical company decisions to reminders about parking lot etiquette and upcoming bake sales.)

Jump ahead to the present. Nowadays, the average in-box is clogged with everything from legitimate executive communications to news feeds, movie reviews, links to funny cat videos, and spam, spam, and even more spam. To the undisciplined, email can devolve into a digital black hole from which you may never emerge. If nothing else, the implied urgency of electronic communication, be it an email or text, seems to warrant an instant response. *But don't be sucked in.* Don't be a victim. There are precious few emails that can't wait a few hours to answer. (For evidence of this fact, consult the Quadrants we discussed in the previous chapter.)

To take the power back in the digital communications realm, you must set reasonable expectations for yourself and the people who contact you. (Remember: Just because someone sends you an email, it doesn't mean they own a piece of your time.) For instance, consider adding a message to your email signature that says something like, "I check my email twice a day: once at 10:30 and once at 3:30 Pacific Time. Emails received after 3:30 will be read the following day," or, "I'm happy to collaborate on documents and files using modern technologies. Emailing revisions via attachment does not fall into this category. Please share Goggle Docs or equivalent modern tools with me so we can collaborate faster and interact in real time." (Yes, people might be taken aback from the boldness of the latter message, but they will soon learn to get with the program if you remain firm.)

Our Final Recommendation: Unplug

When you want to concentrate, turn off your cell phone. Put it in your drawer where you can't see it (beside your now-hidden candy jar). PIMCO founder and billionaire investment guru Bill Gross famously spends much of his time without a cell phone and rarely checks email. He says this allows him to stay focused on his most important tasks at hand. If it's good enough for him, it's probably good enough for you, too. Stick to a schedule for checking email, voicemail, and texts.

SMART Goals

Since this chapter is all about using structure to become a time management hero, we are going to conclude it by covering several different systems for taking back your day. We will begin by establishing benchmarks for success. In his 2006 book, *Leading at a Higher Level,* business management expert Ken Blanchard, author of the best-seller *The One Minute Manager*, advises professionals to establish what he calls SMART goals to structure tasks, thereby defining what needs to get done to stay on track. SMART is an acronym for:

Specific & Measurable: Each goal must be specific, observable and measurable.

Motivating: You must understand *why* the goal is necessary, why achieving the goal is important.

Attainable: The goal must be realistic and achievable within the time you've allotted. (Do not confuse this with *easy*. The great basketball coach John Wooden said, "Your goals should be both difficult and realistic." Remember: Don't be afraid to aim too high and miss. Be afraid to aim too low and hit.)

Relevant: Make sure what you're trying to achieve is actually connected in some way to your larger business enterprise or personal ambitions.

Trackable/Time-Bound: There has to be a time limit, a ticking clock, associated with your goal or chances are you'll never achieve it.

Once you've established your SMART goals, refer to them daily to ensure you are structuring your days for optimal achievement. Better yet, keep them top of mind by continually asking yourself: "How does what I am doing right now contribute to one of my SMART goals?" If you find your activity bears no relation to your SMART goal, it indicates this task is not important and you should cease doing it ASAP in favor of something that does take you where you want to go with your life. One more word of advice: Feel free to revise your list as necessary, but never let establishing these goals ever become just a casual, forgotten intellectual exercise.

Eat that Frog

A major proponent of goals and structure, author Brian Tracy has made a career out of helping people understand what they need to do to get ahead. In his 2001 time-management book, *Eat That Frog*, Tracy presents a philosophy based on primetime vs. downtime prioritization. Though he doesn't explicitly describe it this way in his book, the central idea is that you should do what is hard and what is important as soon as you can to stay ahead of your sometime worst enemy: procrastination. He advises structuring your workday like this:

Write down all your goals for the day. (By the way, you might as well make them SMART goals so long as you are doing this. Nothing wrong with mixing and matching advice from the greats, right?)

2. Label each with an A, B, C, D or E.

A = Very important, serious consequences if not done. Examples: you have to meet with a very important client, pay your taxes, or get your passport renewed for that upcoming trip.

B = Important, but minor consequences if not done. Examples: return a phone call or an email of minor importance; someone may be annoyed that you didn't do it, but it's not the end of the world.

C = Nice to do, but not as important at A or B; no negative consequences if not done. Examples: go out to lunch with co-workers, read the newspaper, or attend a co-worker's birthday party. Anything that is fun to do but really doesn't contribute to your most important goals. Fun fact: Studies have shown most workers spend approximately 50 percent of their time on C-level tasks, so if all you do is eliminate C-level tasks you will double your productivity.

D = Delegate. And how much should we delegate? Answer: as much as we can. Delegation will free you up to do more complex tasks and focus on your own top 20 percent of tasks. Think back to Covey's quadrants—we tend to delegate our Quadrant #3 and #4 tasks and keep the Quadrant #1 and #2 tasks for ourselves. Delegate the Quadrant #1 and #2 tasks wherever you can, especially if you have subordinates who are ready for more responsibility. This strategy is a win/win if you can help others grow and develop in the process.

E = Eliminate if at all possible. Examples: any tasks that have become obsolete, are no longer relevant, or bad habits that need to be done away with. Here's a rule to live by: If it does not have to be done, it has to not be done. (You already have too much to do.)

And if you have more than one A-level task, categorize them as A1, A2, A3—and so on. More than one B-level task will be B1, B2, B3, and so on. The key to this system is to discipline yourself to work on your A1 task continuously until it is complete, then move on to your A2 task until it is complete, and so on. If you are unsure what category your tasks fall into, get your boss involved with your prioritization process and ask him/her to help you prioritize. You would be surprised at how many people are unclear about what their top priorities at work really are. As you can see, Tracy's structure closely resembles Covey's quadrants; however, the difference is that Tracy emphasizes *proactivity*. Or to put it bluntly: get the hard, important stuff done *now*.

Recognizing the reality that when it comes to things falling under the A and B category, there are bound to be particularly difficult tasks—those that are distasteful or otherwise off-putting (but tend to be very important)—he recommends knocking them out early. Why? Tracy is highly aware that the reason people procrastinate so much is they get overwhelmed by "frogs." This is a reference to Mark Twain's famous adage, "Eat a live frog first thing in the morning and nothing worse will happen to you for the rest of the day."

Frogs are the yucky stuff we don't want to deal with but must for our own good. The biggest, ugliest frogs tend to be the most important things we need to do. They also tend to be the things we procrastinate on. Rather than put them off, he advises you to "eat those frogs." Tracy's advice for primetimers, downtimers, and in-betweeners alike is to eat those frogs first thing in the morning to get them out of the way, thereby making room for more interesting, pleasurable, and rewarding activities.

Invest in an App

We have talked a lot about how new digital tools, like email, can inundate us with new problems. But they also can free us if we invest in working with the right ones. The good news is when it comes to effective time management, you don't have to do it alone. There is plenty of helpful technology available. Some Apps I recommend for support include:

Wunderlist: A simple task-management tool for scheduling a to-do list; it's nice because it can be used across a number of devices (desktop and mobile).

Todoist: Speaking of to-do lists, Todoist allows you to keep all of your tasks in one place. An integrative management system, it can be used by multiple collaborators, updating items as they are completed in real time.

Any.do: Another productivity app, this tool is designed to aid with task management. Offering a calendar assistant and grocery list reminders, it can also sync your tasks across multiple devices, including your watch.

Protect Your Staff's Primetime, Too

If you have subordinates, find out when their primetime is. Do you schedule routine, sometimes unproductive meetings at that time? If so, change that schedule. Encourage staff members to protect their primetime (shut their office doors, turn off their phones, or block their calendars for a couple hours a day when they will be at their peak.) This will increase their productivity and they will thank you for it.

Adjust Your Schedule for Peak Performance

Ever come in to the office on a weekend and think to yourself, "Wow, I can get so much more done when nobody is here!" The reason it seems that way is—it's true. You're getting controllable, uninterrupted primetime and we are two to three times more productive under that scenario. If your boss is open to you adjusting your schedule, go for it. You will need to show results, but most bosses want their employees to be more productive, so odds are if you make the request, you will get a chance to prove it works. Whether it's coming in early, later, or on the weekends, explain to your boss that you are at your best at (x) time and you'd like to adjust your schedule accordingly so you can get more done. Even if you only get to do this once or twice a month it's worth it.

Get Your Boss Involved in Your Prioritization Process

Many people spend years on the job thinking what they value is what their boss values, when in reality their boss values something completely different. Don't let this happen to you. Write down your top three on-the-job priorities on a sheet of paper. Put this list in your pocket. Now go to your boss and ask her to write down what she thinks your top priorities are. Take a look at both lists simultaneously. Do they match? Are they even close? If they're not in the same ballpark, that's a problem. From now on make sure you and your boss agree on what your top priorities are. (Even if you don't *agree*, at least now you know where your boss expects real results!)

As we conclude this chapter, I hope it has become apparent the right structure can establish a helpful framework for avoiding distractions and achieving your goals, both personal and professional. But what kind of goals should yu set? And what goals are most likely to lead to happiness? This is the subject of our next chapter.

Action Steps:

In the time-tracking matrix we discussed in the previous chapter, indicate times when you've been interrupted and the nature of these incursions. At the end of the week, add them up by category.

During the following week, use the tips recommended in this chapter to reduce the number and length of interruptions. At the end of the week, add up the interruptions and compare the numbers. Do you see an improvement? What areas still need attention?

Turn off email alerts on your phone *and* computer. You don't need to be interrupted each time something shows up in your inbox. Check your email two to three times per day.

Once before lunch, once before you leave the office, and *maybe* once in the evening. This will minimize interruptions, keep you working on your most important tasks, and best of all, will show you how few emails actually are urgent.

Chapter Three
3—2—1—GO(AL)!

*"Never give up on a dream just because of the
length of time it will take to accomplish it. The
time will pass away anyhow."*
~Dr. Martin Luther King, Jr.

Dangers of Short-Term Thinking

What makes a poor person poor? Why, despite the $15 trillion-plus the federal government has spent on anti-poverty programs since the 1960s, does poverty continue to plague American society? One answer, popular among conservative thinkers, is that the poor remain so because of bad decision-making. Some evidence supports this supposition. According to the American Psychiatric Association, impoverished high schoolers are five times more likely to drop out compared with the general population.

Close to 70 percent of out-of-wedlock births occur among single women earning less than $10,000 a year, according to the U.S. Census Bureau. And the prime market for usurious, high-interest so-called payday loans is the working poor.

Wishing to discern the truth, the prestigious journal *Science* in 2012 published the results of a study exploring links between poverty and decision-making. In it, volunteers played a video game. Each player began with a certain number of resources, usually in the form of time or points. Some players began with more, some with less. As they monitored game play, the researchers noted players who started with fewer resources tended to focus wholly on accomplishing immediate tasks, whereas players who began with greater resources took time to strategize and study the situation before launching into task fulfillment.

The researchers also thought it important to mimic other aspects of our current socio-economic system to more fully simulate life. That's why they introduced credit. If, and, or when players began to deplete their resources, they were offered the opportunity to borrow additional ones—at increasingly escalating costs—again simulating the situation the poor often face when contemplating payday loans to stave off financial ruin. What the researchers recognized is something many social observers and critics realized long ago: it's hard to *come back* from being down and out. As players became increasingly resource-poor, their desperation often caused them to borrow more and more, consequently getting further and further behind.

Rethinking Short-Term Thinking

There are two ways to interpret the results of this study. One is to conclude poverty tends to lead to bad decision-making, not vice versa. The existential pressures destitution puts on people causes them to focus on fulfilling immediate, short-term needs with little thought to their long-term consequences. But what the study also suggests is the poor stay poor *not because they are inherently inferior*, but because there are structural causes for their decisions. Poor people tend to make short-term (bad) decisions based on the pressures of their situations. This leads to an important question: Might we make so-called bad decisions if we, too, lived in bad circumstances?

Putting this question aside, the study also suggests another key insight: Focusing on the short-term is in itself a bad decision, one destined to become self-defeating. Short-term thinking has often been cited as a cause of decline for many American companies competing internationally over the past 40 years. In a landmark 2014 study titled, "Evidence and Implications of Short-termism in U.S. Public Capital Markets: 1980-2013," authors Rachelle Sampson, visiting associate professor of strategy at Georgetown's McDonough School of Business, and Yuan Shi, a researcher at the University of Maryland's Robert H. Smith School of Business, found that focusing on delivering short-term returns to shareholders has caused public companies to fall behind in areas vital to long-term success.

"When firms focus on the short term, they steer profits to shareholders immediately instead of spending money to improve productivity, the greatest driver of economic growth for both companies and our economy," Sampson explained. "They spend less on R&D for the next great products and services, less on capital spending to improve manufacturing efficiency, less on employee training, and less on environmental and community stewardship." A related 2016 article in *The Atlantic*, titled "How to Stop Short-Term Thinking at America's Companies," offered the following data to illustrate the nature of the crisis when companies stop thinking about the big picture:

> The average holding time for stocks has fallen from eight years in 1960 to eight months in 2016.

> Almost 80 percent of chief financial officers at 400 of America's largest public companies say they would sacrifice a firm's economic value to meet the quarter's earnings expectations.

> Companies are spending more on purchasing their own shares to drive stock prices up rather than investing in equipment and employees.

Better Think Long Term

All of this talk about the need for long-term thinking brings us back to the topic of goal setting, which we touched on in the previous chapter. To avoid the perils of short-term thinking and its dangers, it's vital you set long-term goals for yourself. Buying a new car or getting a $10,000/year raise may satisfy some immediate needs, but it won't make you much happier or change the course of your life for the better. Instead, goals like finding a career that makes you eager to get up in the morning, or saving enough money so you can retire comfortably by age 60, or raising a family can set you on the correct life-altering path because you can structure your day-to-day activities and short-term goals as stepping stones towards your bigger, long-range goals.

As we have seen throughout this book, the way toward such success means incorporating the personal and the professional. Going back to Chapter One, we discussed how difficult it is to be happy in your career if your personal life is in turmoil. No doubt you've witnessed office workers whose performance suffered due to relationship issues, problem children, illness, and other personal distractions. Maybe you've even been there yourself. Remember, in Maslow's Hierarchy of Needs, Physiological, Safety, and Love/Belonging support Esteem and Self-Actualization, so you must ensure the first three categories are satisfied before beginning to think about addressing the top two.

Life is a Team Effort

If you are married, it's optimal to also marry your personal and professional goals in cooperation with your spouse. In a marriage, life is a team effort and the only way to make progress is for both partners is to pull in the same direction. Writing for the *Harvard Business Review* in February 2015, spouses Jackie and John Coleman stress the importance of domestic partners working in concert, even when pursuing individual goals.

"Couples in committed, long-term relationships often see each other every day, but rarely plan or set resolutions together," they write. "By not doing so, couples may actually be making it harder to achieve their goals. This January, we fully integrated our personal planning for the year for the first time. We've always informally mentioned our goals to each other, but this time around, we talked with intentionality about why we were chasing those goals, and how we planned to get there. By including each other in the process, we invited the other to not only be aware of what we plan to accomplish this year, but also to hold us accountable as we strive to reach these goals."

This real-life couple suggests setting a date to review your goals together once a year. Establishing such an annual matrimonial board of directors meeting can seem stuffy and awkward at first—not at all something two people might do who share the same bed every night—but it can be immensely helpful. After getting over the idea of it, jump into action. Use this time to reflect on what progress you've made over the past 12 months in various areas; determine which goals you met, which you missed, and, if possible, the reasons for each. Also, discuss how you feel about each perceived success and failure. Were you satisfied by each success or did some leave you unsatisfied? In areas where you fell short, were you frustrated, or did you find yourself not really caring one way or the other?

Once you've reviewed your annual progress report, write out your goals for the year ahead. Maybe your priorities have changed and you want to replace an old goal with a new one. Don't be surprised if your priorities, both personal and professional, evolve as you mature. Why commit these goals to writing? Numerous studies have shown people are far more likely to keep promises and commitments when formalized, be it in a legal contract or just writing them in a notebook. Putting pen to paper makes the abstract real. Last, once you have made your annual plan, consider holding monthly meetings to check in on your progress, both joint and individual. These will not only keep your goals fresh in your minds but allow you to make course corrections as needed.

Exercise: Top 3 Goals, Quick-style!

Here's an exercise to get you started. Set a timer for 30 seconds. Write down your top three life goals before time expires—ready, go! Again, think long-term.

One was probably professional or financial. (Start a business that is both fun and profitable; make $1 million a year; be elected to federal office, etc.)

One was probably related to health/fitness (e.g. Live disease-free; maintain the weight I had when I graduated college; live to 100, etc.).

One was probably relationship oriented (e.g. Find and marry a person I can spend the rest of my life with; have a strong relationship with my children; have a large network of friends, etc.) These tend to be the areas of life that are the most important to us.

Now, repeat the exercise, but give yourself a little longer, let's say five minutes instead of 30 seconds to consider each goal. When you're done, compare the two lists. Are they the same? They probably are. Working fast forces your subconscious to the surface, revealing your true feelings without conscious inhibitions. Repeat this exercise but give yourself different lengths of time to complete it (20 minutes, one hour, etc.) you'll find that what you forced yourself to write down in 30 seconds changes very little, even if you give yourself more time.

Once you have your top three life goals, examine each through Zig Ziglar's *7 Steps for Success*. For those of you unfamiliar with Hilary Hinton "Zig" Ziglar, he was an American author, salesman, and motivational speaker famous for his Southern twang and folksy, albeit aggressive, approach to professional and personal success. His 7 Steps to Success are:

Write down what you want.

Explain why you want each goal.

Identify the obstacles preventing you from achieving the goal.

Identify the people, groups and/or organizations you need to work with to achieve your goal.

Identify what you need to know to achieve your goal.

Develop an action plan to reach each goal.

Set a deadline for achieving the goal.

Do this for each of the three life goals you have selected. Now you have a clearer path to personal happiness. As you embark on this journey, the key to success is to make sure your goals are clear. As you learn new things or your life circumstances change, your goals and priorities may change as well. That's fine, as long as you are taking inventory of your goals while monitoring your progress as well as your direction. Management guru Peter Drucker said it best, "Before you begin climbing the ladder of success, make sure it's leaning against the right building."

Now Use Your Other Team to Reach More Goals

If you have a professional goal, you probably can't achieve it alone. Thomas Edison and Henry Ford didn't attain greatness working alone in their basements. Steve Jobs, Bill Gates, Mark Zuckerberg, and Jeff Bezos didn't change the world alone. They all worked with teams. In some cases, very large teams. The teams worked as a unit even if the leaders reaped the principal benefits. If you own a company, whatever its size, you know how important it is to have skilled, talented and, above all, *motivated* people working for you. The same holds true if you're an executive for a large company or corporation. To obtain your professional goals, you must have the support of your team. And, of course, one of the best ways to enlist your team to support your goals is to make sure you support *theirs.*

What we are talking about here is *buy-in.* In a 2016 Gallup Poll, a record-low 31.5 percent of employees reported feeling engaged or excited at work. This means nearly 70 percent of workers feel bored, unfocused, disassociated, or just plain don't care about the jobs they're doing. This kind of disengagement can be disastrous for a company as a whole and for you personally as a leader or manager. Want to get the best from your people? Want their help to get what you want? Then, you need them engaged.

You need their buy-in.

How to Make Them Come in for the Big Win

Even if you haven't read every worker productivity study written in the past 20 years, you probably understand instinctively that an engaged workforce is a productive workforce. Employees who are eager to work, who pay attention to what they're doing, and who care enough about the outcome to expose problems and propose solutions create better results. Engaged workers are also less likely to quit, minimizing expensive personnel turnover compared with those staff members who just show up to collect a paycheck.

Before "engagement" become a popular buzzword, we used to call this "morale." Strong morale was the sign of a strong, healthy, and productive organization. Poor morale was the sign of a company going down the drain. Armed forces units even dedicated morale officers whose job it was to keep the troops in good spirits. After all, any military putting its service members' lives on the line is undoubtedly expecting a lot from them. When morale breaks down in such crucial situations, big problems occur.

When it came to the Army or other large organizations, old school ways of thinking offered two basic ways to boost morale: the carrot and the stick. The stick represented punishment. The idea held that people worked hard because doing otherwise led to bad things: getting kicked out of the unit, a demotion, a pay cut, getting fired, or at worst, dying. Another way of putting this leadership style? Management by fear or command and control. Conversely, the carrot represented goodies. Rewards. Work hard and maybe you'd get a bonus, a pay raise, even a promotion. The polite word for such an inducement is *incentive*, but you can also consider it a *bribe*.

As it turns out, neither the carrot nor the stick is a particularly effective management tool. Unsurprisingly, constantly threatened employees tended to resent their managers and their jobs. They also became prone to sickness and absenteeism. During the Industrial Revolution the command and control style of management led to widespread unionization and a contentious relationship between management and workers. On the other hand, employees who only viewed their jobs as a means to an end tended to work hastily—sloppily. Incentivized to seek rewards or prizes above all else, many resorted to backstabbing and corner-cutting just to be first to cross the finish line. When a company becomes little more than a competitive cage match like the cutthroat real estate office in David Mamet's classic *Glengarry Glen Ross*, you know you're in trouble.

Today's leading companies have dispensed with the old carrot-and-stick strategy in favor of employee engagement. What this basically means is creating a team-based environment in which workers actually care about the *work itself*, not just salaries, status, or other perks. Fostering the type of work situation in which every employee sees him/herself as a fellow stakeholder breeds greater success. Why? When individuals feel a personal commitment to the organization, they are more willing to put its triumphs above their own.

So how do you create this type of engagement, maximizing the productivity of every team member? The following proven strategies include:

Establish three to five meaningful, measurable and memorable company objectives around which your team can align. (Amazingly, studies show only about 15 percent of companies currently do this.)

Create a collaborative team structure in which each member has a degree of authority as well as the responsibility resulting from such authority. Welcome suggestions, constructive criticisms, and creative solutions. Let each team member play to their strengths.

Set clear expectations. Let each employee know what you expect from them. Set specific goals and timelines but make them realistic and attainable. There should be no ambiguity regarding goals, objectives, and priorities. (A fifth-grader should be able to understand what they are.)

Encourage employees to challenge themselves and get out of their comfort zones. Inspire them to learn new skills and take on unfamiliar tasks, even if these require a learning curve. Multiple studies show the more employees contribute, the more fulfilled they are.

Track your team's progress on a regular basis. Make sure everyone is aware of how the team is doing.

Practice positive accountability. If an error is made, work together to find the cause, developing ways to prevent similar future mistakes. Above all, avoid the blame game, which only serves to put people on the defensive.

Request each employee go through the Top 3 Goals exercise outlined above. Let them know you want them to achieve their goals and are willing to help. This exercise is somewhat personal; encouraging people to clarify their goals shows you care about their well-being, and best of all it only takes 30 seconds.

Get Everyone on the Same Page

Transparency is important when building a strong, cohesive business team. Just as secrecy and hidden agendas can kill a marriage, keeping employees in the dark about company goals, strategies, policies and, yes, financial matters, can be corrosive to team cohesion and engagement. Employees stand to benefit from knowing what's going on at *all* levels of the company hierarchy and the factors leading to major decisions. For instance, if your company is doing well financially, your employees should know why and be congratulated for their contributions. Likewise, if your company is performing poorly, workers should know that, too, and feel free to offer solutions. After all, good suggestions can just as easily come from the rank as the file.

Helpful ways to promote such transparency include holding consistent all-hands meetings as well as regular departmental staff meetings. Remembering what we have learned so far, make sure these meetings are short and sweet. Stick to important issues and topics to avoid never-ending gab sessions. Publishing a monthly company e-newsletter is also an ideal way to make announcements, celebrate achievements, and acknowledge employees who have gone above and beyond.

On the other hand, problems tend to fester when transparency isn't practiced by an organization. When transparency erodes, it is inevitably replaced by conjecture. Nature abhors a vacuum, and when the company isn't providing information, the rumor mill will commence production. And rumors can be deadly to team morale. Once a rumor begins to spread, it can metastasize quickly, hijacking people's imaginations. The solution: Always tell the truth. People can deal with it, no matter how uncomfortable. Rumors, however, are like conspiracy theories; they're dark, insidious, and give rise to suspicion and fear. Bottom line: When a rumor begins, kill it before it kills you.

Create a Team of Self-Starters

Even if true success requires team effort and openness, qualified managers are still needed to lead such teams. Most every manager dreams of heading a group of self-starters, individuals who need only be given a goal and let loose to accomplish it. After all, who wouldn't like to surround themselves with people they don't have to tell what to do all of the time? While such glorious autonomy may appear to be just a wistful fantasy, it's actually easier to pull off than you might think. Here are suggestions today's top business experts offer for assembling a team of self-starting A-Players:

Hire Slowly/ Fire Quickly

Never hire impulsively. Take your time. Do your due diligence. Check references. Review social media posts to learn about your candidates. Use Google to check for stories on their past successes or failures. Make sure your person's temperament and work style meshes with the rest of your team. Conversely, if you find you have a rotten egg in your bunch, remove them quickly before the rot can spread. Poor performers and bad attitudes tend to drag everybody else down with them. Or, as Deputy Barney Fife always advised on *The Andy Griffith Show*, "Nip it in the bud."

Suggested Reading: For more ideas on creative ways to hire and screen candidates, check out former Google human resources director Laszlo Bock's book, *Work Rules!* in which he outlines the hiring processes Google uses. (Each "Googler" interviews with folks from many departments and typically spends six months in the hiring process from start to finish—wow.)

Lead from the Front

The legendary colonial reformer Mohandas Gandhi once said, "Be the change you wish to see in the world." A world leader who once inspired millions, he makes a good point. Be the example you want everyone else in your organization to emulate. Be organized, punctual, enthusiastic, and always follow through.

Deal in Real Time

When a problem arises, talk to the people responsible for it immediately. Never let problems fester. The longer you allow people to wander off the right path, the more difficult it is to get them back on it. Keep it unemotional and to the point "Stop doing *that,* start doing *this,* keep doing *that* —" is a good script to follow. Likewise, give positive feedback immediately. The sooner you say what a great job they did, the more likely they are to repeat that behavior.

Make Sure Everyone Has the Tools They Need

This includes the proper training as well as any actual tools or applications they need to properly execute their job. If someone asks for something, take it seriously. If the answer is "no," give them a good explanation they can understand. Otherwise they will think you just don't care.

Practice the Golden Rule

When I speak to audiences, I am always surprised at how few people are familiar with the Golden Rule. "Treat others the way you want to be treated" is my favorite management principle because you can never go wrong with it. If you are ever in a conundrum, you can always refer to this. Remember, people may forget what you told them, but they will always remember how you made them feel.

Reward Outstanding Performance

Since the dawn of history, organizations have rewarded outstanding performance with some kind of tangible badge of achievement. Even in today's armed forces, officers and enlisted personnel proudly wear medals and ribbons on their chests, earning them respect from peers and civilians alike.

In such groups as the Boy Scouts and Girl Scouts, achievements are rewarded with colorful patches that become part of their uniforms. Athletes struggle for years just to earn a competitive medal or trophy that they may treasure for the rest of their lives. In entertainment, there are no greater status symbols than the Oscar, the Emmy, the Grammy, and the Tony. None of these totems can be bought. They all must be earned.

All of which is to say, there are some incentives that are even more powerful than money. Sure, money is great—it pays the bills—and cash bonuses and prizes are fine ways to reward employees for outstanding performance. However, the buzzlike feelings money produces tend to be short-lived. Very few people frame bonus checks and put them on their walls or in a display case.

Instead of just incentivizing with cash, consider holding monthly, quarterly, and annual awards ceremonies where top achievers are recognized publicly and given trophies of increasing size and value. Run contests in which goals are clearly defined and achievements publicly recognized. Offering an employee of the month trophy someone can proudly display on their desk can do more to boost engagement than a $50 check that's spent and forgotten.

All of this talk about the optimal ways to best incentivize your people leads us to our next chapter on how to truly get the best from your staff. In Chapter 5, we will learn firsthand why the stick approach is a doomed and antiquated form of motivation and how to lead your staff for best results. But for now, let's wrap up with some action steps toward fostering long-term planning and achievement.

Action Steps

Remember, while it's important to set goals, it's just as crucial to monitor your progress and adjust your goals as necessary.

The following are ways to dynamically assess your progress in the long term.

1. Establish a set of future goals that are relevant, achievable and measurable.

2. Take an inventory of your progress every month. Evaluate your progress toward your long-range goals.

3. Change goals as necessary as time goes on. Airplanes have pilots make course corrections as weather, wind, and other circumstances dictate. As you gain new knowledge, don't be afraid to make course corrections in pursuit of what is important to you.

4. Consider if/when it is time to abandon a goal. Is it still relevant? Looking back, if you had to do it all over again, would you? If the answer is "no," then it's time to hit the eject button!

Chapter Four:
Motivate Your Staff

"Motivation is everything. You can do the work of two people, but you can't be two people. Instead, you have to inspire the next guy down the line and get him to inspire his people."

~Lee Iacocca, business legend and former head of the Chrysler Corporation

In our last chapter we spent time exploring employee management and motivation, from the most effective incentives and rewards to the importance of commitment to the work itself (and not just the monetary rewards of working). In this chapter, we'll dive deeper into the question of what truly motivates employees, examining how factors like a company's structure and your own management style can impact your people's engagement and productivity. We'll also introduce specific tools you can use to keep your staff operating at their highest potential.

Types of Leadership

Experts in group dynamics identify four principal types of organizations: Hierarchical (strong top-down), Egalitarian (strong bottom-up), the less common Panopticon (control by unseen authority) and Diffuse (control by independent entities.) Each leadership style has its own pros and cons that can foster or inhibit employee engagement. Let's review each now.

Hierarchical

From the Bible to Bloomberg L.P., hierarchies have been the most common organizational structure for thousands of years. Picture a pyramid with a single, strong leader at the top, giving directives to the people directly beneath them, who then in turn give directives to the people beneath them, and so on.

Military organizations are an obvious example: at the top, you have a commander-in chief (someone like a king, prime minster or president), beneath whom are generals, then colonels, then majors, then lieutenants, then sergeants and, finally, corporals and privates who make up the base of the pyramid. It's the same model used in most ancient kingdoms, in which the king (or queen) served as ultimate authority and servants of varying titles were charged with executing their orders. Today, most large companies also conform to this structure: a CEO at the top, then various senior vice presidents, regular vice presidents, directors, managers and, finally, the staff at the bottom.

Top-down hierarchies are popular because they offer a simple chain-of-command allowing high-ranking members to exert maximum authority on those below them. Or, as many a boss is fond of saying, "This company isn't a democracy."

With an enlightened leader at the top, a hierarchy can be extremely efficient and innovative (see The Walt Disney Studios 1923-1966 under Walt Disney, or Apple 1997-2011 under Steve Jobs). However, efficiency and innovation can suffer when too many layers of authority isolate the bigwigs in the head office from the people who do the actual work. Safely positioned in their ivory towers and surrounded by yes-men, some leaders disconnect from reality and become uncontrollable tyrants (see China during the Great Leap Forward 1958-1962 under Mao Zedong, or Apple 1976-1985 under Steve Jobs).

Egalitarian

The egalitarian (or bottom-up) model flips the hierarchical model on its head, with information, and thus ultimate authority, flowing from the bottom to the top. Think of the classic capitalist edict, "The customer is always right." The buyer, not the manufacturer, is the ultimate authority on what is good and what is bad.

Leaders in egalitarian organizations operate under the assumption the troops on the front lines—be they soldiers, salespeople, or factory workers—have a clearer understanding of the organization's strengths, weaknesses, needs, and direction than the folks at the top of the pyramid. Democracies and democratic republics like the United States ideally operate under the egalitarian model: The people choose their leaders and those in power govern only with the consent of the governed. Communism as envisioned by Karl Marx is another example, with the workers controlling the means of production.

In the late 20th century, many companies experimented with this bottom-up approach to leadership, vesting workers with greater-than-traditional degrees of authority and removing as many layers of middle management as possible. The model did, and still does, work well for leaders primarily concerned with the big picture and comfortable delegating tactical decisions to subordinates.

Egalitarian organizations often excel at fostering collaboration, creativity, and innovation. On the employee side, when workers' opinions are taken seriously and they have direct access to upper management, morale improves and turnover rates are minimized, while in time, a more engaged workforce allows the organizations to be more responsive to changing market conditions.

On the other hand, an organization can reach the point where "too many cooks spoil the broth," losing focus, direction, and effectiveness amidst the chaos of internal rivalries, infighting, division, tribalism, and ultimately, chaos. However, while a pure egalitarian leadership system can prove unwieldy, many companies still utilize some aspects of the model, regularly surveying their workforce for suggestions on how company operations can be improved.

The 2016 book *That's Not How We Do It Here* uses a fable about African meerkats to illustrate the benefits and weaknesses of hierarchical and egalitarian structures. Authors John Kotter and Holger Rathgeber tell the story of the meerkat Nadia, who lives in a well-functioning authoritarian community of rules, traditions, and best practices where everyone is safe and well-fed. Then the rains cease and conditions deteriorate, and the community begins to suffer—especially when the elders in charge refuse to consider new ideas and punish those who question their authority.

Frustrated, Nadia and her friends abandon the community for a smaller colony that welcomes innovation. There, new ideas initially prove so successful that the colony begins to flourish and expand—until it grows so unwieldy cooperation begins to falter and chaos ensues. Realizing a community needs some structure to thrive, Nadia finds a middle ground allowing for creativity, but imposes some basic rules and restrictions to maintain order—much like many companies today that combine elements of both hierarchical and egalitarian leadership models.

Panopticon

Imagine a circular prison compound with a tall tower at the center, shining blindingly bright floodlights on the cells surrounding it so the prisoners can't see who (if anyone) is watching them, while the prison authorities can see everything that goes on. It might sound like a dystopian nightmare, but this panopticon model—in which an organization's leaders are mysterious and unseen—is the way many people believe most governments and organizations actually work. The panopticon model is best exemplified by secret societies like the Illuminati, Priory of Sion, and Skull & Bones. A favorite subject of so-called conspiracy theorists, these groups supposedly are comprised of obscenely rich and powerful families and individuals who secretly pull the strings of power, profiting off war, famine, and every other malady affecting human society while their leaders remain in the shadows and avoid all responsibility for their nefarious actions.

While extremely rare, panopticon-style organizations have existed – and still exist – usually within highly authoritarian societies where the object of government is to keep the population in a constant state of fear and uncertainty. Ironically, some poorly-run companies and bureaucracies can degenerate into what feels like a panopticon: When chains of command dissolve, no one has any idea who is really in charge, and chaos and confusion ultimately reign.

Diffuse

Diffuse structures spread power and authority out among a number of institutions or individuals. Think of the United States government, which not only divides its powers between the executive, legislative, and judicial branches, but also among 50 separate state governments. The Founding Fathers intentionally created this complex system of checks and balances to avoid the kind of concentration of power—and tyranny—common among the authoritarian monarchies of Europe at the time.

Today, so-called multilevel-marketing organizations such as Amway or Mary Kay offer the best model of a diffuse organizational structure in business. These organizations have no employees, just independent contractors, each of whom operate as an independent business entity with the authority to set its own hours, working conditions, etc. While the central authority may set general policy, all tactical decisions are up to the people on the front lines.

The diffuse model gives organizations the flexibility needed to quickly react to changing conditions on the ground. In the U.S., the states are famously known as the "laboratories of democracy," where new ideas and programs can be tested without necessarily impacting the union as a whole. For example, some states have legalized medicinal and/or recreational marijuana, which remains illegal at the federal level. Likewise, companies operating under the diffuse model can better meet the needs, tastes, and demands of their local constituencies.

The downside lies in the lack of discipline and brand conformity a diffuse power structure can permit. The absence of a strong central authority allows individual groups to go rogue, taking actions that may undermine the interests of the group as a whole.

Key Value: The Golden Rule

Ultimately, any of the above leadership systems can be successful provided the leaders within the system are proactive and engaged. One strong, proven strategy is to follow what we already discussed: The Golden Rule: Do unto others as you would have done unto you. In other words, treat people the way you want to be treated.

In the workplace, this means being polite and courteous to subordinates regardless of their station. It means showing appreciation for good work, and when people underperform, finding ways to help them improve. Look for underlying causes, provide constructive criticism, as well as any additional training, tools, or other resources your people may need to maximize performance. Equip your staff with the latest knowledge, strategies and techniques relevant to your industry, and your investment will pay off.

If you're in a position of leadership, especially in a top-down system, think of yourself as a "benevolent dictator." Yes, the company has given you authority over people, but that does not give you the right to make those people's lives more difficult by overstepping your authority. Power should be combined with compassion and sensitivity to others' emotions. Avoid being abusive or insulting, even in high-pressure crisis situations. And if you do step over the line (and at some point you probably will), take responsibility, apologize and do what you can to repair any damage. Remember, your employees have personal lives just like you do, and while their commitment to the job and the company matters, it may not always be the biggest thing on everyone's mind at a given moment. Learning to see things through other peoples' eyes is a skill that will serve you well.

Which relates to the most important thing you can do if you want a happy, productive staff: Show your people you care. Not just to be a good boss, but because research proves it works!

The Hawthorne Effect

The seminal study on what has come to be known as The Hawthorne Effect occurred nearly 90 years ago, in the 1920s. Researchers Elton Mayo and Fritz Roethlisberger visited Western Electric Company's Hawthorne Works in Cicero, Illinois, with the goal of determining how environmental changes affected worker efficiency. Management first briefed the employees on the impending study, during which time they explained to the group of 20 women (yes, they were all women) that, "You are the best and brightest employees at the factory, which is why you were chosen for this study —" then those workers' productivity was monitored as researchers brightened and dimmed the lights, raised and lowered the temperature, played different kinds of music, altered working hours, and changed other conditions. Mayo and Roethlisberger were baffled by the fact that every single change was followed by an increase in productivity.

The researchers had no explanation for the fact that every time they altered something, productivity increased. Dumbfounded and with no usable data, they couldn't make heads or tails of the study and threw their hands in the air. They finally decided to ask the women, "What's going on here, how come every time we change something you increase production?"

What do think the women said? To paraphrase, it went something like this: When you started this study, you told us that we were the best and brightest, and that made us feel special, that made us feel important. Ever since then, we haven't wanted to let you down, we wanted to impress you and maintain that high level or performance, so each time you changed something it reminded us that you're watching and we kicked it up a notch.

What we learn from the Hawthorne studies and numerous studies thereafter is that two things must be present for people to give their best effort:

They need to be watched

They need to feel important

Think about it, this makes perfect sense. When do singers give their best performances? In front of big, cheering crowds. When are records set in sports? In front of big, cheering crowds. Dubbed The Hawthorne Effect, this concept can be applied to virtually any workplace situation. Just by letting workers know their superiors believe they are important, and physically see them working, you can measurably boost both morale and productivity. Ever heard of management by walking around? Keep The Hawthorne Effect in mind—you will always be better served to give people a pat on the back than a kick in the behind.

Surveillance and Micromanagement

On the other hand, paying *too much* attention to workers—micromanaging their behavior to the point of timing bathroom breaks and keeping records of every mouse click and keystroke—can have the opposite effect on employee morale and productivity. For example, Amazon is famous for its ability to deliver anything and everything to your door at lightning speed and at super-competitive prices. Its warehouses are also infamous for being modern-day sweatshops where low-wage workers are closely monitored and pushed to perform with machine-like speed and precision. The result is high employee turnover, frequent accidents, higher-than-normal rates of illness, and frequent bad press detailing dehumanizing working conditions.

Terrorizing your workforce might help your company score magnificently when it comes to simple, repetitive tasks such as filling customer orders. However, creativity and innovation generally need a more relaxed environment to thrive, which could be why the residents of Amazon's executive suite work in under very different conditions than their minions on the warehouse floor. It's also why leading tech companies such as Google, Netflix, and Qualcomm are famous for lavishing their workforce with perks ranging from free gourmet lunches to on-site massages and yoga classes.

Perhaps Mary Kay Ash, founder of her namesake cosmetics giant, put it best in her *Six Right Ways to Lead People:*

No matter how busy you are, you must take time to make the other person feel important.

Everyone wants to be appreciated, so if you appreciate someone, don't keep it a secret.

We treat our people like royalty. If you honor and serve the people who work for you, they will honor and serve you.

God didn't have time to make a nobody, only a somebody. I believe that each of us has God-given talents within us waiting to be brought to fruition.

My goal is to live my life in such a way that when I die, someone can say, she cared.

Criticize the act, not the person.

Deadlines Force Efficiency

Earlier, when we discussed goal setting, we noted that every objective must contain a deadline. It's not enough to say, "Complete the Jones contract;" you have to say, "Complete the Jones contract by 4 p.m.

Wednesday." Only goals carrying some sense of urgency stand a chance of being completed. That's just human nature.

If you're a boss, giving deadlines to other people is easy. It's part of the job. Setting deadlines for *yourself* is another story—because it's just too easy to cheat. A promise made to yourself is the easiest to break. Which is why, even if you're way up at the top of the pyramid, you need someone else to set a deadline for you.

Psychologists Dan Ariely and Klaus Wertenbroch studied the power of third party-set deadlines in 2002 at MIT. Looking for ways to combat procrastination, they assigned two groups of students the same three research papers. One group was free to set its own schedule, while the second was given specific deadlines for all three assignments. The results were predictable. The self-guided students slacked off until the last minute, then scrambled to complete their papers during the final week. Those given deadlines were far more disciplined and productive.

So how can you get someone to set an effective deadline for you if you don't answer to anyone? There has to be something at stake. Consider doing the following:

Announce the deadline to friends, family, or co-workers. Make meeting the deadline a matter of personal honor.

Establish a bet with someone. For example, tell a friend you'll pay them $100 if you miss the deadline. (And if you make it, they have to take you to lunch.)

Create real consequences for failure. For example, promise to give a friend a prized possession, or agree to run naked down the street. Whatever works for you.

How to Eat an Elephant

One reason people avoid deadlines is because big, important tasks, the kind that happen to need deadlines the most, can seem too daunting. It can be hard to wrap your head around the idea of writing a novel or designing a company website, let alone commit yourself to a course of action to make it happen. That's when your only real choice is to eat the elephant.

We are, of course, referring to the old saying, "How do you eat an elephant? One bite at a time." What it means is that even the biggest projects can be accomplished by breaking them down into a series of smaller tasks, each with its own deadline. For example, say you want to write a 50,000-word book. That seems like a big job, the kind you might put off indefinitely. But what if, instead, you broke it down into a series of 1,000-word-a-day assignments? That's about four double-spaced typewritten pages a day, something most professional writers can easily produce in an hour or two. Just by writing 1,000 words—just four pages!—every day, you could have the entire 50,000-word book done in 50 days, or less than two months. Suddenly, the job not only looks possible, but *doable*.

However you decide to break down a project, make sure each task easily can be accomplished within the time frame you give yourself and then stick to the schedule. Don't start pushing commitments back to the next day (as in, "I missed my 1,000 words today, so I'll do 2,000 words tomorrow"). Make your daily goal a habit, something you *have* to complete before allowing yourself to do anything else.

Remove Self-Limiting Beliefs

One key reason we—and our employees—fail to meet our goals is that we are all captives of self-limiting beliefs. We spend our entire lives hearing and reading about what we can and cannot do. Granted, some self-limiting beliefs are well-founded. For example, if you aren't born with amazing lungs and the ability to carry a tune, you are never going to sing grand opera. And if you're a 45-year-old guy who topped out at 5-foot-6, you can leave playing in the NBA off your bucket list.

But there are many other truisms that aren't technically *true*. And they can hold you back from getting what you want. For example, we've all heard the expression, "You can't teach an old dog new tricks." We've been taught to believe learning is for the young, and that the older we get, the harder it is to acquire new knowledge and skills. In fact, numerous scientific studies have shown that while younger minds may be more "plastic" than mature ones, there is never a point at which (barring physical or mental disability) learning becomes impossible. With sufficient training and motivation, people in their 60s, 70s, and 80s can acquire new skills and abilities.

Beware! The idea that you (or a member of your team) have lost the capacity to learn and improve can become a self-fulfilling prophesy. Keep pushing yourself to move beyond your comfort zone. Always be an explorer, an innovator. And encourage the people who work for you to do the same. Ask yourself: "What new skill would I learn if I knew I could not fail? What new thing would I do if I knew I could not fail?" Ask your team these questions as well, then get to work on eating those elephants.

Remember, fear of failure is usually our biggest obstacle to success.

A Final Look at Motivation

Back in 1957, Pittsburgh, Pennsylvania, psychiatrist Frederick Herzberg conducted a landmark research study on motivation—specifically, which factors led to worker motivation, and which led to worker *de*motivation. His results were published in a book co-authored by Bernard Mausner and Barbara Bloch Snyderman.

Herzberg concluded that motivation / demotivation were not extremes on a single, continuous spectrum. They were, in fact, two separate tracks, leading his conclusion to be dubbed the Two-Factor Theory. Demotivation, he concluded, was governed by what he called "hygiene factors:" things whose presence does not necessarily motivate people, but their absence demotivates people. Factors such as job security and good working conditions are examples.

Good working conditions can vary widely, depending on what someone does for a living. Let's take, for example, a positive work environment, or even a comfortable chair, since both of these would be classified as good working conditions. Have you ever worked somewhere lacking a positive work environment? Did it demotivate you? Yes, it did.

The point is that a positive work environment won't necessarily motivate someone to work harder, but the *lack* of a positive work environment will definitely demotivate. Same with the comfortable chair example. If you have a comfy chair to sit in, that isn't going to motivate you to work harder. But if that chair is taken away and you're given a rickety old stool to sit on (in the name of budget cuts) for example, you're going to be demotivated and it's going to drive you crazy! You will talk about it at the water cooler and curse your boss' name if they refuse to replace it. So now is the time to ask yourself, are there any hygiene factors at your workplace that aren't being met? If so, now is the time or action.

Surprisingly, adequate pay is also a hygiene factor. In the 1940s and 1950s when "windfall" pay increases and their effects could be easily studied in factories where production changes could be quickly tracked (on assembly lines, for example), experiments in pay increases and their ability to motivate people took place frequently. What they found was this: Imagine your boss came to you and your team and said, "You all have been doing so well, we are going to double your pay, effective immediately."

If that happened, how long do you think productivity would increase for? A month? A week? A day? Try *one hour*. Yes, a windfall pay increase will increase productivity for about one hour. You see, people get really excited, work really hard, then in about an hour go right back to doing what they did before. What we learned from Herzberg and countless other studies is that the *lack* of money makes people very demotivated, angry, and depressed (no real revelation there). However, while making more money makes people progressively happier, the happiness *bump* starts to level off at around $45,000 to $50,000. While a person making $50,000 will be significantly happier than someone making only $25,000, that same person will be only marginally happier if his/her salary doubles to $100,000.

In other words, once all of your basic needs are met, something else is required to generate true happiness. And as Herzberg discovered, even if you are not dissatisfied at work, something else is required to generate true satisfaction. So, what is that something else? For most people, it's purpose. At work, people are happier when they believe they are doing something important, that their work has meaning, and that their work is being acknowledged and appreciated.

Herzberg called these factors "motivators." They make people push themselves to perform beyond expectations.

They make people willing to experience short-term pain in the service of long-term success. This is why praise, awards, and citations usually produce better results than threats, criticism, or even monetary rewards. A person who is already making enough money to pay the bills can always find a way to rationalize not making more if doing so requires undertaking a task they find boring, aggravating, or distasteful. On the other hand, those same people will gladly throw themselves into projects they find fun, challenging, exciting, or otherwise satisfying, even if no extra payment is offered.

When young Walt Disney was creating what would be the first feature-length cartoon, the movie *Snow White and the Seven Dwarfs*, the production was troubled and its prospects were often dim. Disney famously acted out the entire story to his small, underpaid staff. His creative team was so excited by his vision that they worked long hours, often unpaid, even as the production fell months behind schedule and went thousands of dollars over budget. Their commitment and enthusiasm, despite the odds, resulted in a cinematic classic that launched one of the most powerful entertainment empires on the planet. That's the power of real passion and leadership.

Now that we've discussed leadership and motivational styles, the next chapter will share ways to provide feedback that keeps employees motivated and eager to do more.

Action Items

Identify your company structure. Is it top-down, bottom-up, panopticon, or diffuse? Determine how this affects your leadership style, and if this is, indeed, the best way to achieve the results you want.

Determine how much work you delegate and look for ways to delegate more. Remember, the more authority each employee is given, the more likely he/she is to commit him/herself to succeed.

Scout your workplace for any demotivators that easily can be removed. For example, are people forced to take long lunches and then stay late to make up the time? Are there flickering light bulbs that can be easily and cheaply replaced? Do you follow bureaucratic processes that were started years ago but are no longer relevant? You would be surprised how many demotivators linger in an organization simply because nobody has taken the initiative to try to remove them.

Go elephant hunting. Do you have any big, important tasks that you have been procrastinating on? Can you break them down into smaller tasks and eat those elephants one bite at a time? Use a calendar to schedule smaller pieces of these large tasks and watch how fast you progress towards your goals.

Chapter Five
Good Management Requires
Difficult Conversations

"Nothing in life is more important than the ability to communicate effectively."
~Gerald R. Ford, 38th president of the United States

Managing employees often involves critiquing the work of others. This is not nearly as easy as it sounds. Sure, praise is easy to bestow. It makes everyone feel great. But negative criticism is a minefield. As anyone who has been on the receiving end knows, negative comments of any kind are often perceived as attacks. And attacks can trigger a flurry of reflexive responses. Some people react to criticism by becoming withdrawn, depressed, and apathetic: "Everything I do sucks, so why even try?" Others become defensive and scornful: "You think you can do better? What do you know?"

And still others get just downright hostile: "Oh, yeah? Screw you,"

Since none of these reactions are conducive to doing good work, let's consider how to reframe these conversations.

Strategic Feedback

Providing good feedback, commonly called constructive criticism, requires a professional, skillful, and strategic approach. Empathy plays a large role in being able to put yourself in the employee's shoes, anticipating the emotional response your criticism is likely to elicit. It's also important to recognize feedback serves a major purpose: to improve the quality of the work product. You wish to achieve a desired goal and must therefore give feedback in such a way to achieve this effect. Criticism is just expressing your own emotional response, be it anger, frustration, disappointment, or impatience. It is counterproductive and not in the best interest of either you or your team members.

The best strategic feedback consists of several elements you can mix and match to suit the situation at hand. Plan the conversation out in advance and try to figure out which type of feedback will help your employee grow without sending them away in tears (some people are more sensitive than others). You want them to get something from the feedback, not just hear you as white noise. Try to keep their benefit in mind at all times. It's not the place or time for you to unload your own negative emotions, so stay calm. Author Ken Blanchard once said: "Feedback is the breakfast of champions." Let's go through some techniques now, including what to say and what not to say at different times.

Creating a Cool-Down Time

You may have heard the saying, "Great managers don't delay." Allowing a problem to fester only gives it time to metastasize, to grow into something even more dangerous and destructive. However, knowing how and what to criticize takes thinking and time. If you see a problem, your first instinct may be to address it immediately, but such a reflexive response may preclude you from understanding the whole picture or generating the proper solution.

Take a few minutes to step back, consider the challenge, assess possible tactics, and then approach your subordinate with feedback. Put yourself in that person's shoes. Try to see things through their eyes. What are all the reasons they might have done x, y, or z? Prepare for what they might say in response and have your own responses prepared. Try to stick to the facts, not emotions.

Know Your Goals

Again, providing feedback is not just an opportunity for you to vent. Before offering feedback, have a specific result in mind. What, exactly, is the end product supposed to look like? How are you going to articulate this? What steps are needed to get there? What, exactly, do you want this person to contribute, and how? How does this person learn? Do they need to be told, drawn a picture, etc.? What is the best way to show them what you want? Stick to the facts, not emotions. If you stick to the facts of the situation and the changes you want *based on those facts*, directions will be better received and there will be less to argue about. Remember, we can send an email around the world in a few seconds but it can take much longer for the actual message to travel that last two inches from the ear to the brain.

Ask Permission

Surprising someone with negative feedback can trigger exactly the kind of negative, defensive response you are trying to avoid. Instead, consider asking permission to offer feedback.

The Wrong Way: "No, no, no. You did this all wrong."

The Right Way: "I just looked over your report. Is this a good time to talk about it?"

If not, schedule it for a time when you know you will have enough time discuss. Give the employee a couple options if they are very busy. By offering your employees a choice, you provide them a modicum of power, which helps bring down emotional defenses, opening them up to feedback.

The Caring Approach

Frame your criticism as concern for the employee's well-being.

The Wrong Way: "You turned this report in late."

The Right Way: "The report was due at 5 p.m. yesterday but you didn't turn it in until this morning. Is everything okay? Is there a problem?"

The subtext here is you are concerned for the employee as an individual, not just as a work machine. (By the way, don't just feign such caring. People can see through it. The most adept managers actually care about their personnel.)

Build on Strengths

Assume that in the course of making their first pass, your employee did *something* right. If so, start with that. Put them in a positive, receptive frame of mind. From there, start talking about *opportunities for improvement.*

The Wrong Way: "The design is awful. It doesn't work at all."

The Right Way: "I like what you were going for here, but I think with a little different approach, it could be even stronger."

Never say the work is bad. Just say it could be better.

Be Direct. Be Specific

Most people will accept criticism if presented clearly and explicitly. However, general and ambiguous feedback provides little direction and can make the receiver resentful and uncooperative.

The Wrong Way: "I don't like this paragraph. It just doesn't sound right. Fix it."

The Right Way: "I think the paragraph would work better if you stated your thesis statement at the outset and then rephrased it at the end."

It's best not to leave questions in your subordinate's mind as to what you want. Questions breed confusion. Confusion stops workflow and causes even more problems. Rely on specificity to get things done in a timely manner.

Don't Make Accusations

One sure fire way to make employees uncooperative is to accuse them of wrongdoing. This will inevitably put them on defensive, making the situation contentious. Instead, simply encourage them to do better.

The Wrong Way: "You installed this part all wrong."

The Right Way: "Take another look at the way you installed this part. It doesn't look right to me."

No one likes to be accused of doing something wrong. Framing your critique properly will foster greater trust between you and your employee, leading to better results.

Use Suggestions, Not Commands

Avoid bossing around your people. Unless you're in the armed services issuing commands to subordinates, you'll probably get better results *not* barking orders like R. Lee Ermey in *Full Metal Jacket*.

The Wrong Way: "Fix the document's formatting."

The Right Way: "You might want to take a look at the formatting.

Something seems off."

Most adults shut down when they hear commands. Commands rob people of their sovereignty to make their own decisions. Suggestions, on the other hand, are often well-received if given politely and kindly.

The Scoreboard Method

Sometimes, it is best to just let facts speak for themselves. In sports, merely hearing the phrase, "The defense really blew it," tells the listener little about how the football game was played. Instead, stats on touchdowns scored, yardage gained and lost, percentage of passes completed, fumbles, turnovers, and completed field goals, offer a clearer, far more insightful picture of overall performance.

The Wrong Way: "I am afraid to say, you are not just not doing a good job here."

The Right Way: "Let's discuss some of the problems that have come up in the last few months. They include —"

Ultimately, giving an employee a report card based on their job's metrics not only provides an objective assessment of performance, but also serves as a standard against which subsequent performance can be judged. As the saying goes, "If you can't measure it, you can't manage it." The key is to just state the facts. Think of the scoreboard in a football game. It just states facts: score, time left, who possesses the ball, how many timeouts they have left, etc. It doesn't say, "They should have benched that quarterback in the second half."

Make It a Conversation, Not a Lecture

When providing feedback, allow for a back-and-forth conversation. Ask questions. Allow the employee to respond, provide explanations, ask questions, and even challenge your main premises.

The Wrong Way: "This is what's wrong here and here's how you're going to fix it."

The Right Way: "I understand there have been some issues lately. What are your thoughts on how to fix them?"

Good employees are independent thinkers and may have solutions you haven't even considered. They may have even been restrained from developing better ideas because of the parameters you originally supplied. Talking *with* them—not just *at* them—is the only way to find out.

Ask open-ended questions, get them talking, so you can figure out what they are really thinking. People can be reluctant to share their true feelings with their boss, but you need to foster candor and be the type of person that people can let their guard down with. If you truly care about them as people, your staff will sense this and open up to you more.

Feedback Style Can be Key to Employee Retention

Study after study has shown employees rarely leave jobs; they leave *managers*. Workers in even the toughest and demanding of environments will not only stay, but thrive, when their managers are positive, caring, encouraging, supportive, and empathetic. When employees feel valued, when direction is clear, and feedback is positive and precise, they will give the proverbial 110 percent. Conversely, people in even cushy jobs are inclined to become restless and seek greener pastures when bosses are abusive, negative, dismissive, belittling, insulting, unfocused, or impossible to please.

Timing is Everything

When you give feedback can be just as important as the feedback itself. When are you at your best? What is your primetime? In the morning? In the afternoon? Choose a time when you're alert and sharp. Also, take the recipient's schedule into consideration. Is he/she working against a deadline? Or is he/she between projects?

Choose a time when the recipient is likely to be open and receptive and not distracted by other priorities. Midmornings and midafternoons tend to be the best time for feedback meetings. This allows everyone to get settled and their heads in the game. Pushing the meeting to right before lunch or right before quitting time, especially late in the day on a Friday, only invites restlessness and distraction.

Treat Your Employees like Adults

How often have you heard a boss refer to his company as "my family"? Suggesting a company, even a huge corporation, feels like a family elicits feelings of warmth, loyalty, caring, and belonging. The danger can occur when bosses take this metaphor literally, casting themselves as authoritarian parental figures and their employees as children who need to be micromanaged—and, when necessary—disciplined. Such a heavy-handed approach can lead to rebellion.

Michael, my co-author, experienced this firsthand when working at a mortgage company during his first job out of college:

"I was one of about 20 to 25 guys who made a living cold calling prospects about refinancing their mortgage," Michael explains. "We thought we were living out the movie *Boiler Room*. There was a lot of rowdy machismo in the air. And like a frat house, the office was pretty much a mess. Even though everyone had a waste basket at his desk, which was emptied every night by the building custodian, we tended to let food wrappers, soda cans, and discarded paper either pile up on our desks or get tossed casually onto the floor.

"Like I said, it was a mess. Anyway, the bosses got sick of us not cleaning up after ourselves, but instead of just talking to us as adults about cleanliness expectations, they decided to 'teach us a lesson' by taking our waste baskets away.

"Now we had to dispose of the trash ourselves, walking down three flights of stairs to visit the dumpster—in the middle of a Missouri winter. So, what did you think happened? Did we shape up and keep the office clean? *Of course not.* Not only did the office get even messier, but because our bosses treated us like children, we stopped respecting them and grew to resent them. We greeted every new order or directive with the same derision we had for their 'brilliant' waste basket idea."

Bottom line: When giving feedback, always be clear about your expectations and treat your employees like adults. Because they are.

The Medium is the Message

As media analyst Marshall McLuhan famously stated back in the 1960s, "The medium is the message." The manner in which you transmit your feedback can say as much as the feedback itself. When providing criticism, choose the medium that is not only most convenient, but also the likeliest to have the greatest impact and resonance with your receiver.

There are four basic ways you can communicate:

Face-to-face

Conducting a live, in-person meeting is, by definition, the most personal. It also offers the greatest opportunities for empathic interconnection. Numerous studies have reported the majority of communication occurs from non-verbal speech elements. These include volume, tone of voice, eye movement, and body language. Each element can express if you are angry, hostile, concerned, eager, or disappointed, regardless of the words you use. When conducting a face-to-face feedback meeting, it's best to do it in private, even when providing positive feedback. No one likes to be dressed down in public. It's humiliating and breeds resentment. Even complimenting people in public, especially doing so repeatedly, can peg the recipient as the teacher's pet, leading to inter-office resentments.

Video conferencing

If you and your employee are not in the same physical location, video conferencing services, such as Skype, FaceTime, and Zoom, offer a virtual face-to-face meeting in which facial expressions and body language can still be part of the conversation. These services also allow for screen sharing, which can be critical when referencing specific charts, reports, or other documents. On the downside, the quality of such meetings can vary due to factors such as local Wi-Fi strength and bandwidth, as well as the technical acumen of the parties involved. "How do I turn on the camera?"

Phone calls

If you want to go old school, telephones—mobile or land-lined—are always available for manager/employee conferencing. Though they allow for convenient two-way conversations, they necessarily lack the often-critical non-verbal elements of person-to-person communication. Use phone calls for employee evaluations and feedback if you must, but recognize it's not the optimum way to promote empathy.

Emails

Providing employee feedback via email may seem cold and impersonal, but it serves two important functions. First, it provides the employee with a specific, written record of your comments and suggestions so there can be no misunderstanding, and, if necessary, a formal action plan to follow. Second, it provides you with a paper trail in the event you are considering firing the employee and need to protect your company from a possible unlawful termination, harassment, or discrimination suit.

When planning to provide employee feedback, use the above medium or combination best serving your needs. Having a face-to-face or phone conversation (so people understand your emotions, see it in your face or hear the tone of your voice) then following up with a written record so that important items are not missed or forgotten may seem redundant, but it can guarantee your story is heard and the details recorded.

This strategy is more time-consuming but it dramatically reduces the potential for misunderstanding and is a very good technique for anything complex. Remember that in emails, minor punctuation changes such as underlines, bold letters, highlights, ALL CAPS can take on vastly different meanings so be careful when trying to convey an emotional message via email. Emails are good for quick questions, scheduling, or exchanging factual info in a few sentences. Face-to-face or telephone will almost always be the better option for anything that might get emotional.

Power in Numbers

If you need to correct a major ongoing problem, you may not want to do it alone. Consult with other managers. See if they are encountering similar difficulties and learn how they are handling them. Corrective measures may require a concerted group effort.

Similarly, one great way to improve team cohesion—and to even learn something valuable in the process—is so invite your workers to provide *you* counter-feedback. Ask them to critique your performance, your methods, and your results in a group setting. Make sure they understand you expect the same of them as they do of you. They need to be specific, constructive, and offer positive alternatives.

Consider hosting these counter-feedback meetings on a regular basis. You'll get a clearer understanding of our own performance and perhaps learn ways you can improve your management style. And your workers will get a better understanding of how they are being evaluated and may choose to up their game accordingly. If you really want some honest counter-feedback, let your staff do so anonymously. Make it known that you are looking for honest counter-feedback and they can write you a note or give them a survey to fill out.

Explain that you are seeking ways to improve and won't retaliate if they have criticism. Give them the option to tell you face-to-face (no anonymity) but if they wish to submit anonymous counter-feedback, you would appreciate the honesty. They will see you are serious about being a better leader and appreciate your efforts.

Employee Training Pays Off

Too many companies prefer to keep training time to a minimum. They want employees who can hit the ground running and become productive and profitable on Day One. Unfortunately, this sink or swim strategy usually fails to bear fruit. Every company has its own unique way of doing business, its own ethos, and its own style. And this creates a learning curve.

One of the best ways to obtain the best results from your team is to train them properly in the first place. Continuing education and training improve outcomes further, fostering not only enhanced competence but also creativity and leadership. Even an experienced professional can feel adrift in a new environment with new managers, new co-workers, new processes, and new expectations.

Those organizations that take the time to thoroughly train their employees usually find it to be money well spent. The same goes for providing continuing training and education. Some employers believe advanced training actually weakens their position because it provides employees with assets they can use to secure better positions with other companies and often direct competitors.

But while it's true some employee turnover is inevitable, most companies realize that improving their staff's skillsets, and thus expressing trust and confidence in their tenure, is a great way to prevent such defections in the first place. Arming employees with the most up-to-date skills and knowledge is also vital to maintaining competitiveness and relevance in the marketplace.

Remember, Training is a Process

Want the best from your people? Then, it pays to be patient. No one becomes a competent performer, let alone an expert, overnight. Learning takes time and mistakes are part of the process. As Henry Ford put it, "Even a mistake may be the one thing necessary to a worthwhile achievement." Or as Thomas Edison is supposed to have said (in one of many variations), "I never failed. I simply discovered 10,000 ways not to make a light bulb."

Good managers expect their personnel to fail on occasion. They recognize the value of trying things that don't work. At the very least, it means their people are trying. Legendary General Electric CEO Jack Welch is fond of relating how as a young chemical engineer back in 1963, he literally blew up one of the company's facilities in Pittsfield, Massachusetts. After the incident, which fortunately had no casualties, the company's head, Charles Reed, summoned Welch.

Instead of firing the young man for his costly mistake, Reed used the Socratic Method. He asked Welch a series of questions to understand the chain of events leading to the explosion to learn how it could have been prevented. "Never kick anybody when they're down," Welch said, explaining how his boss handled the situation correctly. "Kick them when they start to swell instead of grow, and whack 'em when that happens."

Today, America's top tech companies, including Google, Amazon, Apple, and Netflix, openly encourage their employees to stretch themselves, to experiment with innovative ideas, processes, and concepts. The leaders of these organizations know well the only way to make breakthroughs is to test boundaries, to explore dead-ends, and to, on occasion, blow up a laboratory.

After each failure, you can do what Charles Reed did: employ the Socratic Method to help workers identify what they learned and how to use this knowledge to produce better future results. As part of your process, consider asking the following questions:

What was your mistake?

What did you learn as a result? What will you do differently moving forward?

Observe the 2 R's

Good managers observe what is commonly known as The Two R's. These are Realism and Responsibility. To be a realistic manager means to accept the world as it truly is; not just your workers' strengths and weaknesses, but also your company's assets and resources, your place in the competitive market, and the power of basic business principles.

Employing realism means letting go of "magical thinking," or the idea if you believe in something hard enough, it will happen. The world doesn't work that way. Realistic managers understand the basic principle of Chaos Theory: Any sufficiently complex system is inherently unpredictable. Yes, you should take actions to improve your *chances* for success, that improve the *probability* you will succeed, but there are no guarantees. Or as author Robert Burns so eloquently put it:

"The best laid plans of mice and men often go awry."

The second "R" is Responsibility. This means, in the current vernacular, owning it. Or in the words of President Harry S. Truman, "The buck stops here." Making excuses, blaming others, or just lashing out avoids responsibility and only hobbles your chances for success. As young Jack Welch realized, it's okay to say, "I failed," as long as you try to learn why and take proactive measures to improve your next attempt.

Now that you've learned how to provide constructive employee feedback, it's time to learn the secret to time management: Getting the people who work for you to actually work *for* you. I'm talking about delegation, which is the subject of our next chapter.

Action Steps:

There is a BETTER way to give employee feedback. Use the below acronym the next time a difficult situation occurs with one of your subordinates.

Breathe and wait until you're calm
Evaluate the situation
Tell a colleague, get advice
Throw together/tailor your scoreboard

Engage with your employee

Review and assess your own performance

Before we conclude this chapter, here is another piece of advice: evaluate your team's strengths and weaknesses; where are your best training opportunities? If you could send people to any type of training, what would that be? With online options, the possibilities are truly limitless. Do you have a budget for training? Can you get one? Maybe not today, but sometime in the next year or two? Create a long-term, strategic plan for training if you haven't already. The old saying is still true: Some managers may be reluctant to pay for training, thinking "What if I train my staff and they all leave?" But what if you don't train them and they all stay?"

Okay, one more last thing: Take an accurate assessment of your work environment and adopt your communication style accordingly. Is it high-stress, high-consequence? My wife is a nurse and deals with life-threatening situations in close quarters daily with her co-workers. In that environment people will yell at each other when there is no time for explanations, and it is accepted as normal. Ever watch a boat captain yell at deck hands? Normal. Ever seen how first-responders such as police and firefighters handle a tense situation? They often give curt, direct orders. Again, normal, especially in life-and-death situations when adrenaline is high. Bottom line: Not every workplace is the same so make sure your communication style is appropriate for your circumstances. The way you typically behave *away* from the workplace may not always be what is needed to perform well on the job.

Chapter Six
Become a Delegation Jedi

"You can't do it all yourself. Don't be afraid to rely on others to help you accomplish your goals."
~Oprah Winfrey

In a classic episode of the early 1950s sitcom *I Love Lucy*, Lucy and her best friend Ethel Mertz get jobs at a local candy factory. Their task is simple: As individual candy pieces roll down a conveyor belt, they are to wrap each in tissue paper. They take their positions and the belt begins to move. At first, it moves slowly. The women can comfortably grab the pieces as they come down the line and wrap them in paper.

"This is easy," Lucy remarks giddily. Then, almost imperceptivity, the line begins to accelerate. Suddenly, the women realize they're falling behind. Increasingly desperate, they begin pulling candy off the line, hoping to get to them later before finally resorting to stuffing the incoming pieces in their pockets and in their mouths. And then, just when it appears they will be completely overwhelmed, the line abruptly stops.

The supervisor is coming! In a wild panic, they stuff the remaining candy into their shirts and hats, then into their mouths. When the supervisor arrives, the conveyor belt is empty. "You're doing splendidly," she declares, only to turn to the backroom and shout, "Speed 'er up!"

The look of horror on Lucy and Ethel's faces is one for the ages.

If you believe focus, determination, discipline, and hard work will get you ahead of your work load, you are deluding yourself. As Parkinson's Law puts it, "Work expands so as to fill the time available for its completion." The more work you complete, the more work will be thrown at you. Finish one obligation, and you'll get even more. It's a never-ending cycle. In fact, there is only one time in all of recorded history when all the work needing to be done was actually done. And this, according to the Old Testament, was at the end the Sixth Day of Creation. It's been all uphill from there.

If you want to avoid ending up like Lucy and Ethel on the candy assembly line of your personal and professional life, you have but one option: delegate. You must empower the people who work for you to actually work *for* you—to take some of those candies off before the whole conveyor belt comes crashing down.

Just What is Delegation?

To many people, delegation simply means giving orders. But delegation is about more than just being the boss. It involves taking everything you're particularly good at: your talents, your skills, your knowledge base — and teaching it to others. It means handing a large amount of what you consider your responsibilities over to those you have trained.

Delegation is not the same as hiring specialists to handle tasks you cannot. An entrepreneur who hires a superstar chef to create a menu for a new restaurant is not delegating; this individual is obtaining expertise they do not otherwise possess. On the other hand, if the superstar chef subsequently hires a *sous chef* to actually execute the menu he has prepared instead of doing it himself, this is delegation.

Importantly, delegation does not mean abdicating responsibility. It also doesn't mean handing the work off to someone else and then walking away. To the contrary, when you delegate, you must still supervise the work others are doing and take ownership of the final outcome. After all, any job you delegate is, for all intents and purposes, still yours.

Successful People Delegate

"If your business depends on you, you don't own a business—you have a job. And it's the worst job in the world because you're working for a lunatic!" wrote Michael Gerber, author of *The E-Myth Revisited*. Throughout Gerber's book, he makes a case for a "systems-approach" to business, handing over work to others so as to breed productivity—and foster sanity.

According to Gerber and many other experts, delegation is efficient and cost-effective. It also breeds growth and innovation. One would be hard-pressed to name any great inventor, entrepreneur, or business leader who never delegated. Top attorneys inevitably utilize assistants, researchers, investigators, and paralegals to prepare cases for them. Of course, this is work they could do themselves *if* they had the time. But doing this grunt work is not the best use of their talents and training, so they delegate it to others.

Along similar lines, if you have ever watched an episode of *Mad Men,* you've surely recognized a complex orchestration of tasks in the name of creativity and commerce. Top advertising professional Don Draper often focuses on developing high-level campaign strategies and themes before delegating the execution to people like Peggy, his copywriter, Sal, his designer, and a host of other technicians who perform the assigned tasks to bring the campaign to fruition. Likewise, 30 years ago, computer games, another creative endeavor, were often programmed by just one or two individuals. However, today's games are so complex—requiring tens of thousands of labor-hours to complete—it would take an individual literally decades to finish a job if doing it alone. Delegation is the only alternative.

So Why Don't People Delegate?

So, if delegation is such a wonderful practice, why don't people do it more often? There are all kinds of reasons. None of them good.

They don't trust their subordinates

You've no doubt heard the expression, "If you want something done right, do it yourself." Most people have a high opinion of their own abilities and a distrust of others'. They fear that if they hand tasks to subordinates, it will be done wrong, late, or not at all. This attitude not only is an insult to your subordinates, but also calls into question your own hiring ability. If you don't trust your own people, why did you hire them in the first place?

They want to save time

Giving instructions takes time. Training takes time. Supervision takes time. As a result, you're apt to conclude it's just quicker and easier to do a job yourself. This is short-term thinking. While it may, in fact, take precious minutes to show a subordinate how to handle a particular assignment, this effort may also be an investment in future productivity. Once trained, the employee will be positioned to take on similar future assignments with far less preparation.

They don't trust their subordinates' commitment to quality

You care a great deal about your work product and see your results as a reflection of your own worth and value. At the same time, you may suspect your subordinates are just there to earn a paycheck and are eager to dispense with an assignment as quickly and as effortlessly as possible, quality be damned. Which means you'll probably have to go back and fix everything yourself, so why bother delegating in the first place? Again, this begs the question, what kind of people are you hiring, and why? You shouldn't be working with people you don't trust.

They want to feel indispensable

Some people feel if they delegate work to others, it undermines their own importance to the organization. They want to be regarded as uniquely valuable and indispensable. If other people are doing the work, then they can't claim it as their own and will be less for it. This is a mistaken way to view your personal worth. Most of the time, delegation allows a job to be done faster, better, and more efficiently. If you can make this happen, you have something else to be proud of.

They're loners

Some people just like to work alone. They're partly introverts, partly control freaks. They may even have what is commonly called an artistic temperament. Such people may be excellent technicians (defined as a person skilled in a particular discipline) but make lousy managers. In most workplaces these people should be delegated *to*, not delegated *by*.

They feel guilty

Finally, there are those who feel guilty about delegating work to subordinates. They feel they are abusing their positions of power, foisting unpleasant tasks on others who will resent them for doing so. While such a moral sense may be admirable, such people must be taught delegation is central to a good manager's job; any good subordinate welcomes the chance to contribute, and only by delegating can one train the next generation of leaders.

In short, there is never a good reason not to delegate. So now you've decided to do so, the only question is:

Who to Delegate to:

If you work for a small organization, you may have a limited number of people to whom you can delegate. But if you work for a large company or have a half-dozen or more direct reports, then your options are greater. People who are prime candidates for delegation include:

Employees already skilled in the task at hand. Obviously, employees already possessing experience with the work involved should be first in line for delegation. This not only saves you training time, but also makes it more likely the job will be done right the first go around and won't require as much fine tuning in subsequent iterations.

Employees who need to be challenged. You may possess underutilized employees, those who have expressed boredom with their usual assignments. If so, delegating some of your work to them may be a good way to stretch their abilities, enable them to learn new skills, and add value to your organization.

Employees who need/can handle additional responsibility. Sometimes, you see in employees potential they don't even see in themselves. These people aren't necessarily bored or restless, but nonetheless possess skills and potential not yet utilized. In such cases, delegation can be a good way to get these folks out of their comfort zones, forcing them to exercise skills and talents until now have remained hidden.

Employees who are not already overwhelmed. There may be workers within your organization to whom you can delegate because you recognize that they can take on additional work without falling behind. It's a good idea to seek out these individuals because they have shown an ability to multitask projects without feeling overwhelmed. Once you've seen how they handle the more involved workload, you may wish to consider how they might fare leading others they can then delegate to.

Employees who enjoy learning new skills. The best employees are those who constantly challenge themselves; those who are eager to learn new skills. They will welcome the opportunity to take on new work and learn new things.

What to Delegate

Now that you've given yourself permission to delegate, you may wonder just what assignments you can hand off. While it's a good thing you have a new delegation mindset, be careful. Not all tasks are as delegation-worthy as others. One of the best ways to determine what can be delegated is to consider the work in terms of the Covey Quadrants we discussed earlier. Here's a quick recap:

Quadrant #1 is Urgent & Important. These are tasks that must be done NOW or things will go to hell fast. Examples include: hitting major project deadlines, delivering products to anxious customers, meeting company payroll.

Quadrant #2 is Important but Not Urgent. These are tasks with significant long-term impact, but not pressing; it's possible to take your time. Examples include: long-term strategic planning, routine bookkeeping, employee performance reviews.

Quadrant #3 is Urgent but Not Important. These are the "fire drills" companies often suffer panic attacks over—things that seem critical but are ultimately of little or no long-term consequence. They include tasks like answering "urgent" emails and phone calls, helping a co-worker out of their own Quadrant #3 task, and stopping work to handle any of your other typical interruptions.

Quadrant #4 is Not Urgent & Not Important. These are the true time-wasters, routine tasks and diversions that are part of everyone's day. They often include reading the news, responding to needless phone calls and emails, and posting social media updates.

Unfortunately, most managers' instinct is to delegate jobs in Quadrants #3 and #4 Urgent but Not Important and Not Urgent & Not Important, to their subordinates, keeping the truly important and weighty tasks for themselves. At first glance, this makes sense. Better to unload the routine and distracting jobs off on others and then focus your energy on the tasks of true long-term consequence. But this is a mistake. You should also be delegating jobs in Quadrants #1 and #2. This is where you *need* other's help to make deadlines, to add value and strength to important projects. Only truly important projects can help your workers gain skills, experience, and expertise to be leveraged for future projects. You're not going to build a team of A-Players by sending people out for doughnuts.

Why Delegating is Good for Morale

As noted above, delegation helps employees gain new skills and experiences. But there are other emotional and psychological benefits delegation bestows as well. These include:

Increased Self-Esteem

Putting trust in people improves their sense of competence and self-worth. You're telling them, "You're smart and capable enough to do many of the same tasks I do." This is likely to lead to improved loyalty and productivity.

Increased Pride in Job.

There is a pride in authorship elemental to the human ego. If you have ever signed an original painting or affixed your company's nameplate to a manufactured product, you know what I'm talking about. When people participate in creating something of value, especially when their contribution is substantive and meaningful, it further binds them to their job and increases the odds they'll want to contribute to future projects.

Improves Employee Loyalty and Retention

Did you ever have a job in which a supervisor ignored you or just gave you busy work? How did it make you feel? Probably restless. Undoubtedly, you thought about pursuing alternative employment. We all know menial jobs are dead-end with little or no opportunities for growth or advancement. By delegating important assignments to subordinates, you avoid the trap of sapping your people's morale. Giving your employees opportunities for growth, plus the skills and experience to improve their lives will inevitably better your organization as well. And lead to long-term team players!

Avoid These 8 Delegation Errors

Like any important professional activity, delegation is a learned skillset. It also contains inherent dangers to be avoided. Here are eight of the most common delegating errors to avoid:

Confusing Delegating with Training

Training means providing workers with new skills and methods for executing tasks. Quality training may make your people better at their jobs and even allow them to take on new, more taxing assignments, but if this training isn't taking work off *your* plate, then it isn't delegating. And it isn't helping you.

Not Prioritizing Tasks

Again, when delegating, it's important to focus on the Quadrant #1 and Quadrant #2 tasks, those offering the greatest rewards and the most serious consequences for failure. The Pareto Principle, which we discussed earlier, suggests 20 percent of all your workday tasks will fall into this category, while 80 percent will not. Focus on the top 20 percent.

Being Vague

When you delegate, you need to be clear about the task you are assigning. Crystal clear. You need to tell the subordinate everything required to complete the job properly, including:

The expected outcome in specific, measurable terms.

The project deadline, plus any deadlines for individual project components.

The resources at their disposal, and any limits to those resources.

Any special tools or applications needed to complete the task.

Names and contact information for other people on the project and their relationship to the assignment.

Where and in what form the final work product is to be delivered.

Picking the Wrong Person

Not everyone is right for every job. You know your workers' skillsets, styles, and temperaments. Look for the person who will be the best fit for the job at hand. Don't try to force square pegs into round holes.

Not Providing Enough "Wiggle Room."

In most cases, delegated assignments won't go as quickly or as smoothly as if you did them yourself. It's important to plan for this. When preparing to delegate a task, create a timeline with enough wiggle room to account for unforeseeable problems, errors, additional training, etc. You may want to keep this information close-to-the-vest, giving your assignees an accelerated schedule while keeping the real schedule to yourself. In the best-case scenario, the job is completed ahead of schedule. In more likely scenarios, you miss the false deadline but still have enough opportunities to fix things before the real one occurs.

Being a Perfectionist

Early in the classic 1954 movie *The Caine Mutiny*, tyrannical Captain Queeg (Humphrey Bogart) explains his command style: "There are four ways to do things: The Right Way, The Wrong Way, the Navy Way, and My Way. Do things *my way* and we should all get along just fine." It's long been said perfectionism is the enemy of progress. Trying to get people to do things exactly as you would do them yourself is a recipe for disaster. No two fingerprints are alike, and no two people will approach or execute a task exactly the same way. When you give people responsibilities, let them handle them as they see fit. Otherwise, you're going to get resistance, push-back, and maybe even a mutiny.

Not Monitoring

At the same time, you don't want to give your workers complete free reign. After delegating a job, you need to monitor its progress and get regular status reports. If people are having trouble with certain tasks, you need to know this immediately so you can provide timely solutions. The last thing you want is to discover you have a major problem and there's no time left to fix it.

Not Sharing the Credit

People who contribute to a job's success want to share in its rewards. Bonuses and accolades should be shared with all contributors based on the proportion of work they contributed to the effort. Hogging all the glory for yourself is no way to build team cohesion and loyalty, but it will definitely breed resentment.

Avoid these common delegating errors, practice the proven managerial principles we outlined earlier, and you should find yourself with not only more time to focus on the truly important tasks, both at work and at home, but better outcomes as a result.

Action Steps

If you have issues delegating, think about why. Determine if delegating would actually help you perform your job better.

Identify your three or four most important/pressing assignments using the Covey Quadrant. Resolve to delegate as much work as you possibly can from Quadrants #1 and #2, while working to eliminate items from Quadrants #3 and #4.

Identify two or three people to whom you can comfortably delegate. Write a pro/con list for each. After identifying their likely weaknesses, consider ways to minimize these deficits, be it through additional training or other means.

Once you have received their work back, evaluate the results and how you can delegate better the next time.

Chapter Seven:
It's Never Too Late to Be Productive, Happy, and Successful.
Start Here!

"Never get too busy making a living that you forget to make a life."
~Dolly Parton

When your life is out of whack, everything suffers. Spend too much time at work and your personal relationships pay the price. If you're married, you and your partner are prone to grow distant. Schisms appear. Conflicts become more frequent and more consequential. Alienation leads to hostility. If you have children, they suffer as well. Kids without two present and available parents tend to underperform in school, suffer problems socializing, are more likely to experience depression, and often run afoul of the criminal justice system. Likewise, problems at home inevitably lead to problems at work, and the vicious circle worsens and worsens.

Remember our discussion about airline emergency oxygen masks at the beginning of this book? What I was trying to point out is your responsibility to yourself. Just like a freaked out suffocating passenger struggling to hold it together, you need to take care of *your* needs before you can possibly take care of someone else's. If you don't help yourself, you won't be in any kind of shape to assist others.

The good thing about modeling behavior, though, is the way it too can become like a circle, only not a vicious one. Proper modeling begets a positive cycle encouraging others' emulation. Once you put your life back in balance, there's a greater chance those around you will follow. Your family. Your friends. People you care about. Your fellow business partners or managers. Your employees. You become their model for success. By witnessing the positive changes you make in yourself, they see what's lacking in their own lives and begin creating necessary improvements.

But finding such balance is not easy. It takes time and effort. Remember when you were young and just learning to ride a bicycle? Time and again you'd tip over, falling to one side and then another. You'd frantically turn the handlebars this way and that, desperate to stay upright. No doubt you earned yourself a fair share of scratches and bruises along the way, but eventually you discovered how to center yourself and you were on your way.

Professional athletes take this kind of experiential learning to a higher level. Acrobats practice for years to learn how to tightrope walk or balance atop a giant ball with seeming ease. Surfers must likewise spend months, if not years, acquiring the muscle memory necessary to stay upright atop a fast-moving wave. All of this is to say this book is but one more tool in your arsenal. It is meant to help, but real—and lasting— change must come from you. *From within.* All of the instruction and encouragement in the world can't help you achieve balance. You must find it yourself through actual practice; through trial and error. And you have to be prepared to suffer a few cuts and bruises along the way.

However, with time, patience, and determination, it can happen. It *will* happen. And you will be better off for it. So will your organization. And so will your family. (Believe me. I know firsthand.)

The 21-Day Challenge

How long will it take you to achieve your new life-balance work habits? Those who have studied personal development suggest the average time it takes to develop new and lasting habits is 21 days. That's three weeks. It takes this long to cast off not only old ways of thinking, but also bad reflexes and compulsions accumulated over the years. By being proactive and committal you can develop positive new compulsions that will ultimately become habits. The good news is three weeks isn't long at all. If you follow through with the teachings of this book you will be well on your way to developing a whole new successful mindset in very little time.

Here's what you need to do to make this happen now:

Review the chapters in this book. Pay particular attention to completing the action steps at the end of each chapter.

Identify the Top 3 Goals you want to achieve in your personal and professional life. Write them down. Put them someplace you can easily see them throughout the day. Evaluate your progress on a regular basis.

Identify areas of your life needing improvement and consider ways to fix them.

Allow the people close to you: your spouse/partner, children, co-workers — to know what you are doing and why. Make them part of this process. Encourage them to participate, using the same principles to balance their own lives.

Invite your family to a brainstorming session where you propose ways to restructure your lives so everyone can achieve the work-life balance they need. Do the same with your co-workers.

Be ready for your life to change— for the better!

Q & A: **Questions and Actions**

Before concluding this book, I thought it would be helpful to offer some questions and actions in response to challenges I have received from others dealing with work/life balance problems. Perhaps you are going through something similar? If so, I hope my responses help you just as I hope this book offers a better path in your journey through life.

Q. How do I structure my day so I'm the most productive?

A. Track your mental and emotional states on an hourly basis to determine your personal primetime and downtime. Then schedule your most important tasks, your Quadrant #1 and Quadrant #2 duties, for these periods. At the same time, schedule your less important tasks, your Quadrant #3 activities, for your natural down periods. Try to eliminate Quadrant #4 timewasters altogether—or at least shift them to non-work hours.

Don't check email continuously throughout the day. Turn off those alerts that ping on your phone and computer each time someone sends you a text or email. Check these *only* a couple times per day (preferably during your downtime) and you will avoid wasting time with unimportant interruptions as well as the extra moments you lose getting yourself back on task.

Q. What if my co-workers continue to interrupt me with non-essential issues?

A. First, explain to them your new time-management system, what you are trying to accomplish, and how they can help. If this doesn't work, establish formal times each day when you're available to talk. If even this doesn't work —and especially if people are camping out in your workspace — physically remove them. Not by kicking them out, but by removing extra chairs in your office or suggesting they accompany you on your walk to the bathroom or to some other location. Nine times out of 10 they won't actually accompany you into the bathroom. If they do, you may have some other kind of problem on your hands.

Try non-verbal signals: Shut your office door from time to time. If you feel guilty about doing this, first try partially shutting it. It will have the same effect and send the same message: Do not disturb! If you have no walls and work in a high-traffic area (this is good for administrative assistants) you can use different signals such as small, colored flags on your desk. You will need to explain the new system and get others to buy into the concept, but it works like this: If you are going to be busy working on an important project, raise a small red flag on your desk, which means please don't disturb me unless it's an absolute emergency. This method only works if everyone buys-in and works best if many people use it companywide.

Q. What if I work for a boss who continuously interrupts me and won't relent?

A. Present him/her with a business case for why your new time-management schedule will benefit the company. Offer at least three measurable goals that you hope your changes will achieve and when you expect to achieve them. Show him/her your new management style will be beneficial to the organization and not just yourself.

Q. I'm so busy that my wife is complaining we don't spend enough time together, but I can't seem to get away from work because we are slammed. If I sacrifice my time at work, I'll fall behind. If I sacrifice any more time with my wife, she'll kill me! What should I do?

A. Schedule some time away from work with your wife *alone*. Fly your relatives in from out of state to babysit if you have to. Your spouse is the most important person in your life and you can't sacrifice that relationship. Schedule a vacation where you're gone for *at least* three nights.

This is the minimum time you'll need to recharge your batteries. Certainty, more nights away is better but try to spend at least three nights away from home to get optimum recharge time. Schedule it six months in advance if you have to. Also, pay for it in advance so you can't easily reschedule. Your spouse will see the effort you're making and she will thank you for it.

Q. My family and I have so many things happening on the weekends with kids' soccer games, community activities, chores to do, etc. that the weekends seem as busy as the work week! What can I do?

A. Schedule time to be spontaneous. That's right. This sounds counterintuitive but pick at least two weekend days (Saturday or Sunday) each month when the kids don't have soccer games and you aren't obligated to barbecue at the church social. Then block those days out on the calendar and *don't schedule anything.*

You need to schedule your non-scheduled time or else other activities will inevitably appear to fill the void. Use those days to take it easy, go to the park, or do whatever random thing your kids want to do. It doesn't matter what the activity is, you are just going with the flow and using this time to reconnect with those who matter to you most.

And if you have any extra money, use it to have someone else mow your lawn or trim your trees so you can spend more free time with your family. Remember, no matter how successful you are at work, the quality of your relationships with those closest to you will determine how happy you are in life. Remember: You can always make more money, but you can't get more time!

Made in the USA
San Bernardino, CA
06 February 2020